I Can't Stop Eating

How to break free from the cycle of bingeing

SARAH DOSANJH

ISBN: 978-1-9163432-0-7

First published in 2020

Disclaimer
Although the author has made every effort to ensure that the information in this book is correct at press time, the author does not assume and hereby disclaims any liability to any party for any loss, damage, or disruption caused by errors or omissions, whether such errors or omissions result from negligence, accident, or any other cause. This book is not intended as a substitute for the advice of medical professionals, including mental health professionals. The reader should regularly consult a health professional in matters relating to his/her health, and particularly with respect to any symptoms that may require diagnosis, medical or psychological attention.

*This book is dedicated to
my father, Manjit Dosanjh.
Thank you for giving me the
courage to jump.*

Contents

This book introduces a new way to find freedom from overeating. I call this the RALIC method and it is designed to be self-administered. Approach the RALIC method cautiously if you are living with active trauma. If you have vivid experiences replaying with overwhelming and intense emotions, don't do this alone; preferably work with a trauma-informed professional, but if that's not available, you could consider working through the method with a trusted person who will be able to keep you grounded and connected with the present moment.

If you are someone who is living with an active eating disorder, you may find the ideas in these pages helpful, but this book is not intended to replace professional help, or to be used instead of accessing appropriate treatment.

Introduction

I wonder what prompted you to buy this book and what it is you hope to find within these pages.

The attitude and intention we bring to anything we do have a huge impact on the outcome we get. For example, if you scroll through the social media feed of somebody you actively dislike, you're not likely to see any posts that will change your mind about that person. The intention, even if you're not aware of it, is probably to confirm the negative opinion you already have of them. They could be posting photos of themselves building orphanages in Africa and still you would roll your eyes and cynically wonder why they felt the need to brag about it. However, if you visited their social media page because you really wanted to like them and if you were honestly searching for something to like, you would find what you were looking for; it might simply be a photo of a dog and you'll think *How nice – animal lovers tend to be good people.*

Likewise with this book. If you are consciously or unconsciously seeking to confirm that you are helpless and hopeless, if breaking free from overeating sounds impossible to you, you could find a way to use this book to support those beliefs. My intention is to convey a message of hope, so if hope is what you're looking for, chances are you will find it within these pages.

I believe you can break free from the compulsion to overeat and I believe that it doesn't require iron willpower to do it. In fact, believing you simply need more willpower is part of what keeps you stuck. As Kelly McGonigal points out in her book *The Willpower Instinct,* you don't need willpower unless there is a conflict of will. If you are struggling with compulsive overeating, you are caught in an unwinnable dilemma. Part of you wants to control your eating in order to lose or maintain weight; the other part of you wants to eat without restriction. So far you haven't been able to resolve this with your current thinking, but once you do resolve the inner conflict, you become free to make choices. If you have picked up this book, chances are that overeating no longer feels like a choice anymore – it feels like a habit or compulsion that you can't seem to break, no matter how hard you try.

I know how that feels. I've been there. I know what it's like to be in physical pain from eating too much and yet still feel like it's not enough. It was never enough for me. The more I tried to control my appetite, the more out of control I became. There was always this big, seemingly disproportionate binge eating reaction to every attempt I made to gain control of my food intake. It became my daily battle.

Today I am a psychotherapist on a mission to end the insanity around food and weight. If this book has caught your eye, I imagine weight and body shape are big concerns for you. I hear you. Many people think they have a weight problem, but that is the problem – they think they have a *weight* problem. Your weight is an outcome of your behaviour, plus your biology. The issue isn't your weight – this is simply the outcome you deem to be unacceptable. Weight may be an issue for you, but it isn't the issue.

So what is the issue?

The problem is your relationship with food. Not even your diet, but the way you interact with food on a daily basis. It's the way you think, feel and behave when it comes to making food decisions, and then how you judge yourself for those decisions. All those failed attempts to change the way you eat will have made your relationship with food an increasingly difficult one. Fear and anxiety about how and what to eat lead to a disconnection from your body's signals. The more you try to take control, the more out of control you feel.

I have written the book that I would have wanted to read when I was feeling out of control around food. This book contains what I needed to know back then. The ideas I will be sharing with you are based on my own recovery, as well as from being in the privileged position of helping others to break free from compulsive eating.

Before we begin, let's come back to the idea of setting an intention. What do you want to get out of this book? The way you approach the content, and what you are hoping to gain, will influence your ability to use these ideas to bring about real change. The concepts I will be sharing are tools that need to be taken off the page and into your life, in order to escape the control food currently has over you.

Only you can do this.

But I will be here, cheering you on, believing in you.

PART ONE

⌘

What Lies Beneath

Chapter 1

Everybody Overeats

'First we eat, then we do everything else.'
– M.F.K. Fisher

Let's start by getting one thing straight – everybody overeats. If you look it up in the dictionary, overeating simply means to eat too much. But how are we supposed to know what 'too much' is? Some people think they've eaten too much if they're feeling uncomfortably full; others decide they've eaten too much if they have exceeded a certain number of calories and there are those of us who feel like we have eaten too much simply because we ate something we promised ourselves we wouldn't.

If their weight is going up, many people will conclude they must be overeating. They may try to eat less to literally balance the scales. Certainly, that's what society expects us to do. How dare anyone not want to make their body smaller? That's what everyone wants, right?

Most bodies are resistant to undereating and they rebel by increasing hunger hormones, which in turn forces the brain to think about food. Just as feeling angry will push your brain into thinking angry thoughts, feeling hungry causes your brain to think hungry thoughts. This is why food restriction is inevitably accompanied by food obsession. Your body's complex hunger and appetite systems are designed to make you think about food. Add this to the mental deprivation of not allowing yourself to eat what you want and it's a perfect recipe for out-of-control, or even frenzied, overeating.

You know your eating behaviour is having a negative effect on you, but it may feel impossible to stop it. It doesn't seem to make rational sense, but we see this self-sabotaging behaviour everywhere and not just with eating; there are the other usual suspects too, such as alcohol, drugs, gambling and sex. Compulsive behaviours are all around us and technology has introduced us to a new load of them. People are compulsively working, watching TV, checking their phones and posting on social media. These behaviours can be part of what we consider to be a 'normal' way to live (whatever that means), whether it's catching up with friends over a bottle of wine, posting baby photos on Facebook for faraway relatives, or joining in the office sweep when the Grand National comes around.

Cakes are symbols of occasion and celebration in many cultures. Eating a slice of cake is something most people would do, but if someone eats ten slices of cake, suddenly eating cake doesn't seem so harmless. So at what point does the behaviour become harmful? Where do you draw the line between 'normal' and 'compulsive' cake eating? Is it at two, four or eight slices? Perhaps it's more about perception and consequence – at what point does eating cake make you feel out of control, ill and miserable?

If everybody overeats, it is not so clear cut when it turns into a problem of compulsivity. I would say it becomes an issue when your eating causes you distress, misery, anxiety or depression, or when you feel out of control and your perceived value as a person is being negatively impacted by how you're eating. It's a problem when you judge yourself harshly and when you feel so uncomfortable and disconnected in your body that you can't help but view your body as too big and not good enough.

Notice I am very much focusing on the psychological experience. It always starts with the mind. Focusing on weight as the main problem is rarely helpful and tends to get in the way. Also, physical health as a goal doesn't seem to work very well for a lot of people. Physical health and wellbeing come from the compound effect of all your decisions over a period of time. This is why it isn't a good motivator. In those moments when you're struggling with your eating, having a salad or a plate of doughnuts for lunch today won't make much difference to your health in the long term. You tell yourself you can binge now because you'll make better choices tomorrow. You think *What's the point in making a choice now that's based on physical health when past experience tells me I'm going to blow it anyway? I might as well do it now.*

What and how much we eat have become linked with personal morality. This is nothing new – fasting and virtue have been bedfellows for thousands of years. The problem with this good vs. bad attitude towards food is that it has become entwined with our value as a person. Overeating has become shrouded in so much shame that it has become difficult for people to talk about. For many, overeating is a private experience; a time to withdraw from people's gazes in order to eat. Many of my clients who are in larger bodies won't eat certain foods in public for fear of judgement from others, but they also grapple with a great deal of self-judgement too.

The reasons why we overeat

What would you say if I were to ask you very simply, 'Why do you overeat?' I ask this question a lot and I have heard a whole myriad of answers in response. Notice what came up for you when you read that question. What you tell yourself about why you overeat will have an effect on how you experience your appetite. How you experience your appetite then has a big influence on how you eat. These, or variations of these, are the most common answers to the question, 'Why do you overeat?'

'I have absolutely no idea.'

'The only way my mother showed love was through food.'

'I'm just weak and have no willpower.'

'I have bad habits.'

'I eat because I'm bored.'

'I can't cope with life.'

'I don't know how else to handle my feelings.'

Take a moment to notice what pops into your head when you try to find a reason for your eating struggles. I ask people why they overeat, not because I expect them to necessarily know, but because I need to understand what they are believing about it. What we believe creates our truth, and our truth is everything to us – it affirms our identity and shapes our reality. We are willing to behave in some pretty self-destructive ways to protect the image we hold of ourselves.

If you think you know why you overeat, I'm not here to convince you that your reason isn't true or valid. What I am suggesting is that there could be many more factors at play than you realise. For example, if you believe the reason you overeat is because you have no willpower, you will keep putting your focus and energy into trying to find ways to build up willpower. You'll keep berating yourself and getting more frustrated when you don't succeed. What if one of the reasons you overeat is to escape the feeling of failure? Your belief that you need to find more willpower may not be the answer, and it may even trigger more overeating. When it comes to what may be driving our overeating, we don't know what we don't know. Maybe you're overwhelmed and food is keeping you calm and helping you to cope with day-to-day stresses. You may not want to look at these other possibilities if you are so invested in the not-enough-will-power theory.

There may be things going on that we don't want to be true, so we deny their existence or minimise their impact on us. Our identity hates to be challenged. When something is so far removed from the way you see yourself, or the way you want to see yourself, it's easier to push it away and decide what you need is to just do better. You search for another food and fitness programme to tell you what and how much to eat and you chase the fast results. Because you are seeing physical evidence of change, you think it must mean you're doing really well. Fast results will mean you'll soon be able to emerge as the version of yourself that you were supposed to be all along. After all, when you have achieved your ideal physique, then life can really begin. I might call this your WAIT problem; you are waiting for something to change and using your dissatisfaction with your weight as a reason for putting happiness on hold.

If you are looking for a quick fix, this book is not where you are going to find it. If you don't get down to the deeper stuff driving your overeating, the war with food and weight will rage on. If you tackle your over-desire for food, your weight will settle where your body wants it to be. The body is very wise. We will be going deeper into how we can reconnect with our body's wisdom so we become more self-regulating when it comes to what and how much to eat.

Interesting research is coming to light through the 'Health at Every Size' movement, which indicates that weight is not necessarily a helpful way of assessing someone's health. Our behaviours and circumstances give a much clearer picture of our overall health. Things like processed food consumption, activity levels, the quality of our relationships and our socio-economic status are far more indicative of health and longevity than our Body Mass Index (BMI).

The 'Big Four'

Because overeating shows up in many ways, it's important to understand the differences between the main types of problematic overeating. I'll say it again, everybody overeats sometimes, but throughout this book, when I use the word 'overeating', I am talking about the 'Big Four' – impulsive, compulsive, emotional and binge eating. There may be one of these that stands out immediately for you, but it's usually a combination, if not all of them, happening at once.

There is a lot of overlap between these types of eating. Although binge eating is also a type of compulsive eating, you can compulsively eat without it being a binge. You can also impulsively eat emotionally. An episode of overeating could even be an impulsive and compulsive binge that was emotionally-driven or, what I might call, a quadruple whammy.

Binge eating

Binge eating means eating a large quantity of food in a relatively short space of time, often to the point of physical discomfort. There's a sense of losing control and this can be a very distressing experience.

A binge might involve eating an objectively large amount of food – thousands of calories – or, a binge might be two regular-sized chocolate bars that feel like a lot of food to you. Whether it's objectively or subjectively a lot of food, you feel as if you have lost control and the episode will be followed by unpleasant emotions such as disgust, disappointment and self-loathing.

As with most things, it's on a scale. Perhaps you are someone who has the odd binge here and there, or maybe bingeing is a regular feature in your life.

Binge eating is a component of both binge eating disorder and bulimia nervosa. The main difference between these two eating disorders is that bulimia involves compensatory behaviours (vomiting, laxatives, over-exercise), whereas binge eating disorder doesn't. But I have noticed that a lot of people with binge eating disorder do plan compensatory behaviours, such as telling themselves they will eat less tomorrow or trying to diet.

Bingeing is actually a natural response to deprivation, or perceived deprivation. Even if you are ready to give up on yourself, your body is going to fight for you by triggering the binge response. Be honest with yourself – when you are not bingeing, are you trying to diet or control your food in some way? If so, this restrictive mindset may be an important piece of the puzzle. I have worked with clients whose bingeing behaviour lessened significantly when they gave up trying to diet and this sometimes happens even before any emotional work begins.

Here's the other crucial piece of information – your brain can anticipate scarcity. This means you may not be undereating at all, but the mere thought of restriction can trigger a binge. This is sometimes known as 'last supper eating'.

Let me share a typical example that you might be able to relate to. It's Friday and you are planning to start a diet on Monday. Perhaps you've heard about the high failure rates of diets so you tell yourself that it's not a diet, but healthy eating, or a lifestyle change. When Monday arrives, you have decided you will quit sugar for good. You've been eating too much of it lately so you've decided you're only going to eat whole foods from next week, just the way Mother Nature intended.

Does this situation sound familiar, making promises to yourself about how you are going to solve your 'weight problem'? If so, you know what happens on Saturday and Sunday. Remember, this is your last weekend of allowing yourself all those sugary treats, so it doesn't matter what you eat now because you won't be eating that stuff come Monday. You must have it while you can, so you throw yourself into two days of last supper eating. You eat believing you'll never be able to eat like this again, working your way through all the sugary foods you are planning to give up on Monday morning.

By Sunday night you feel sick as a dog, which only confirms that sugar is terrible for you. It reminds you how bad this way of eating makes you feel and how tired you are of feeling this way. Right now, you are feeling pretty positive about the changes you are going to make tomorrow.

Now it's Monday morning. Your body has been working extra hard to restore homeostasis after the weekend's excesses. You've been riding a blood sugar rollercoaster for the last few days and your taste buds have been overstimulated by the highly palatable foods – foods that have been engineered to stimulate the reward pathways in your brain in a way that 'regular' food can't compete with. That spinach omelette isn't looking like such an appealing breakfast right now, but you eat it anyway, deriving very little satisfaction. It actually tastes like cardboard after the flavour overload of the weekend.

By the time the afternoon dip arrives, your head feels cloudy and you can't quite remember why you thought this was such a good idea. Now it seems a bit extreme to give up all sugar. You long for a little something to pep you up. You start thinking that perhaps today wasn't the best time to start your new regime. You remember that you've got a colleague's leaving party tonight, so maybe write today off and start afresh tomorrow? Yes, tomorrow makes more sense. Well, in that case, better squeeze in a bit more last supper eating while you can.

At my worst, I was engaging in last supper eating every day. Every night I would swear to myself that I would 'do better' tomorrow. In my mind's eye, tomorrow's food would be made up of soups and salads.

But tomorrow never came.

Every day I would fail to meet my expectations. When I lay down at night, I would convince myself that somehow I would be able to do tomorrow what I hadn't been able to do today.

And I fell for it.

Every. Single. Time.

You know Einstein's quote that insanity is doing the same thing over and over and expecting different results? Well, that was me. For a long time I was slowly losing my sense of sanity. I was waging a war on food and despising my expanding body. It was a war I had no way of winning, but I wasn't ready to call a truce yet.

It would be misleading for me to claim that your binge eating will effortlessly stop if you simply avoid mental and physical deprivation. It might, but for most of us there are more complex emotional and cognitive factors at play, which we will look at in more depth over the next few chapters. However, you can do all the therapy, you can address all your underlying issues and obstacles, you can heal every relationship and change the way you see yourself, but if you are still triggering the deprivation response by restricting, or planning to restrict, the bingeing WILL continue. These are strong physiological forces you are playing with. Mess with them at your own risk. Your appetite is like a protective animal; try to cage it and you may wake the beast.

Compulsive and impulsive eating

At a glance, compulsive and impulsive eating look quite similar, but they are not the same. Impulsivity means acting on an urge without any forethought whereas if you are in the grips of compulsivity, it will feel as if you don't have a choice, and it's as if you are acting against your own will. Compulsion is an irresistible urge and impulsion is an unreflective one.

Impulsive eating is when Brenda at the office announces there is cake and you go and grab a piece without considering whether you actually wanted some. The good news about impulsive eating is that, as a standalone, it can be managed by a bit of planning and by paying attention and being present with food.

Compulsive eating is a different beast. It's not about a lack of education; compulsive eaters know the harm it causes to their health and mental wellbeing. They tend to be more informed about nutrition than the average GP. This knowledge often works against them, but I'll come back to this later on.

Beating compulsive eating requires the willingness to be present in your life. This may sound simple, but how often are you really aware during your day? How much time do you spend worrying about what's going to happen, or ruminating over what's passed? Thoughts of food start to creep in and, if compulsive eating is a pattern for you, your brain will have become very adept at knowing exactly what thoughts to present to you to get you to act on the compulsion to eat.

It's a form of self-deception. The moment you believe you need to act on the compulsion, you become convinced that this feeling isn't going anywhere unless you give in to it. It's only afterwards when you 'wake up' from the trance, that you can see how you deceived yourself...again. Over time this creates mistrust towards yourself, which is a scary, unsafe way to live. Becoming more aware involves developing the ability to recognise the thoughts and urges without being compelled to act on them. This is hard to do without first shifting some of the emotional blocks and loosening the old beliefs that keep you stuck.

Impulsive eating is a bit easier to manage. It starts with making a commitment to notice your choices. Tracking food for a while works very well at reducing impulsivity because it builds some awareness, but it may not be a good move for you if you tend to associate tracking your food with dieting. If you have historically found tracking food to be very uncomfortable, and if you find yourself giving it up when you've had a 'bad' day, there is probably a lot of shame and self-judgement going on. This shame makes it very hard to change. You don't want to become more self-aware about your eating because it's too painful to look at it, but it's only painful because of what you are making it mean. Change the meaning and you'll change the experience.

If, whenever you overeat, you make it mean that you are weak and that you'll never be able to change, you'll keep yourself trapped in the cycle. Full disclosure up front – I will be preaching about the importance of self-compassion and curiosity throughout this book. I do this because it works! It changes your experience of the problem, which opens up new possibilities and choices. This will free you up to make actual changes to how you take care of yourself.

Emotional eating

I once heard a life coach say that every time you eat when you aren't physically hungry, you are engaged in emotional eating. I would agree up to a point, but I think this is a reductive way of looking at the role of our emotions when it comes to how and what we eat.

Primarily, we need to eat for energy and to keep us alive. However, eating when not physically hungry could be a sensible response to knowing that you won't have the opportunity to eat again for a while. This is my issue with the hunger-fullness diet, which preaches that you should only eat when you are physically hungry and stop as soon as physical hunger disappears. Physical hunger cues normally subside after a few mouthfuls, so this strategy doesn't work for a lot of people. If you stop the moment you are no longer hungry, your hunger is likely to reappear an hour or two later.

Feeling satisfied after eating is more than just relieving physical hunger. Saying food is just fuel is like saying sex is just for reproduction. It misses out all the many functions food (and sex) can provide, such as pleasure, bonding, love, connection, grounding, routine, ritual and soothing. Emotional eating becomes a problem when it is repeatedly used to try to fill a hole. Food may take the edge off an uncomfortable feeling but often it still feels like something is missing. This is because food can't meet the original need that triggered the uncomfortable feeling in the first place.

Feeling lonely? Eat something.

Angry with your partner? Eat something.

Dealing with bad news? Eat!

Most people can relate to emotional eating to some degree, but it may be much harder to try to explain compulsive or binge eating to someone who has never experienced it. My client Casey said to me, 'I know people can see that I must have a problem with eating, but I struggle to say that I binge eat. I think it sounds so much worse, so I just tell them I eat my feelings and laugh it off. They sometimes say they can relate to that and I think *Jeez! You have no idea what you're talking about!'*

Eating something has the ability to change your physical state in an instant. Eating helps soothe anxiety. You are, in effect, saying to your body, 'Hey, it's okay. I wouldn't be eating all this food if we were in danger, so you can chill out.' By filling yourself up with food, you force your body to start its digestive work and this produces a calming effect.

I like the analogy of an empty crystal glass. If you flick it with your fingernail it makes a clear reverberating sound, but if you fill the glass with water and do the same, you hear a soft thudding noise. The glass is like your body and the water is like food. If you fill yourself up with food, you are able to deaden the emotional vibrations.

Since becoming a therapist, I have noticed that we humans are far less rational than we like to believe. Rationalism is a highly regarded quality in our society, perhaps for good reason; being rational provides safety and a sense of order. Imagine the leader of a country throwing away rational thinking and making important decisions based entirely on how they feel in the moment. When this happens, it's a dangerous situation.

When we see rationalism as the goal, we end up frustrated when we judge our emotions or behaviour to be irrational. This throws us into a conflict because we can't seem to understand our behaviour at the rational level. It feels very important to come up with an answer so that we can fix whatever it is that's gone wrong. I wonder how you try to rationalise your struggle with food. Many of us turn inward and make it mean we must be defective. We move into self-blame. *I must be the problem. I'm bad, weak, defective, not good enough* etc.

While this is a miserable position to occupy, it's no wonder this is where we end up. Just as we see in children, the propensity to self-blame is actually the most hopeful position to take. *If I'm the problem, maybe I will be able to do something about it. If the problem is inside of me, perhaps I have some control; if the problem is outside of me, God help me.*

⌘

Chapter 2

Your Body, Your Home

'Perfectionism is not a quest for the best.
It is a pursuit of the worst in ourselves, the part that tells
us that nothing we do will ever be good enough,
that we should try again.'
– Julia Cameron

Every morning I used to wake up and with a sinking feeling, I would remember that I was fat. My body had expanded so quickly that almost overnight nothing in my wardrobe fit me anymore. I would see people who I'd seen only a few months before and I would register the shock on their faces as their eyes took in my bigger body. My weight gain wasn't slowing down either and I was frightened it would never stop. I saw myself house-bound and bed-bound, like one of the people on that TV Show, *My 600-lb Life*.

This sounds a bit dramatic to me now, but this was how I felt at the time. My body changed so fast that it didn't feel like mine anymore and my mind couldn't keep up with what I was seeing in the mirror each morning. My reflection kept taking me by surprise and I lived in a state of misery, confusion and fear. My thoughts would swing from being hopeful and determined one moment, to catastrophic and despairing the next.

That fear drove me to bulimic behaviours. At first, I justified it as a means to simply feeling a bit more comfortable after a particularly bad binge. At times the discomfort of bingeing made it hard to breathe and I wouldn't be able to sleep. Being sick seemed to undo some of the consequences, but I knew this now meant I had switched from binge eating disorder to bulimia.

For many years I wouldn't accept my body, I couldn't. I was determined that it had to get back to the size it was before my eating disorder took hold. Only then, I believed, would everything be okay. I just had to find a way to get back to the beginning and it would be like starting over afresh. I looked at my life before my eating disorder through rose-tinted spectacles; this current nightmare would finally be over if I could just go back to then.

Looking back now, I can see how my focus on returning to the past kept me stuck where I was for so long. What I really needed was to make peace with my body in order to move forwards and recover. I didn't want to acknowledge that it wasn't possible to undo what I had done. It took a while to admit I had been irrevocably changed by the experience of having an eating disorder. There was no going back, I had to press forwards.

It was with a great deal of initial reluctance that I finally acknowledged and accepted the correlation between my eating and the way I felt about my body. I thought I felt bad about my body because of my bingeing, but it was probably truer to say that I now binged because of how I felt about my body.

I had been broken and defeated by the daily struggle against my seemingly insatiable appetite. History was showing me over and over again that I was fighting a losing battle. Finally, I was done. I knew plenty of women who had enviable body shapes and yet they were desperately unhappy with the way they looked. This helped bring me to the conclusion that how I saw my body had to be the most important thing and I recognised that this was something I did have some control over. My bigger body wasn't objectively hideous; that was just my subjective view of it and now I was ready to reassess.

It would not be truthful to claim I never have a moment of poor body image, but I always find my way back to baseline, which is an attitude of gratitude and acceptance. Also, I just don't think about my appearance as much these days. I look at people in my life who do not meet society's standards of beauty and I think about how wonderful they are, so I choose to assume these people feel the same way about me, regardless of my size.

Is your weight holding you back?

If you struggle with any of the overeating 'Big Four' and you're reading this book, it's very likely that you aren't happy with your body. This might range from mild dissatisfaction all the way up to, and including, body dysmorphia. I want to be sensitive to the different levels of distress that poor body image can evoke. If the way you feel about your body takes up a lot of mental energy and causes you immense pain, trust me, you are not alone.

You cannot know what others see when, or rather if, they notice your body. My clients will tell me that they know what someone is thinking about their weight. They see contempt or judgement in a look, or in the way someone treats them, and they think they know it is because they are being judged on their appearance. Shakespeare wrote, 'The eye sees all, but the mind shows us what we want to see.' I might change the word 'want' to 'expect' (yes, I am rewriting Shakespeare!). We see what we expect to see. If you think you have gained weight and you are feeling bad about yourself for it, you will project that onto the outside world and search for confirmation of what you are believing. You won't notice the first three shop assistants who smiled and said hello; you'll fixate on the fourth one who was rude and then use this to reaffirm to yourself that people would treat you with more respect if you just lost the weight.

You may be living in a body that is bigger than what our culture promotes as acceptable, so it's important to add, if you are living in a bigger body, you may be facing some very real prejudice out there. This infiltrates into the workplace (people in bigger bodies are more likely to be passed over for promotion) and medical care (they are not offered the same treatment options as a patient in a smaller body). You may have been subject to abuse in the street by strangers. I do find the fact this actually happens is an extraordinary thing and it's difficult for me to get my head around it. It's happened to the majority of my clients who live in bigger bodies.

My client Rachel told me she was leaving the gym one day when a man in the street shouted at her, 'You're fat!' She said that part of her didn't care, she *was* fat, but at least she wasn't an arsehole like him and yet, another part of her wanted to shout back at him, 'I'm at the gym! I'm doing what I'm "supposed" to be doing. What more do you want from me?!'

We live in a fat-shaming and fat-phobic culture. Why is it generally accepted that people can be naturally thin, but not that people can be naturally fat? We don't assume that every skinny person isn't eating enough, so why assume every fat person is eating too much? In a society that lauds thinness, we have children as young as six trying to make their bodies smaller by attempting to eat less. Their bodies are growing and they are being taught not to trust their own hunger signals, but to follow some external guidelines about what and how much to eat. At the time of writing this, WW (formerly WeightWatchers) has just released a weight-loss app for children! I despair!

Every child is different, with varying energy needs from one day to the next. They experience growth spurts at different times to their peers and I strongly believe our fat-phobic attitudes are harming our children. Teaching them that they need to follow external eating guidelines, regardless of whether their body says otherwise, is a huge responsibility to place on little shoulders. Mark my words, we are churning out a generation of disordered eaters.

The mind/body connection

Let's come back to you. What if I were to ask you to tell me three things you like about your body? I often put this to my clients and I've asked the same question to other therapists during my workshops. Some people struggle more than others to come up with an answer. They may say something small and specific like their ears, nails or eyebrows. Others may select something bigger and tell me they like their arms, face or calves.

I wonder what popped into your head. The thing that fascinates me about doing this is that, so far, only one client has given me an answer that wasn't about how their body looks (this client was a dancer). I don't specifically ask for things related to appearance, but it doesn't occur to people to think of an answer based on what their body does, rather than what it looks like.

I have the most fun putting it to other therapists at my workshops. I get everyone to write down the three things they like about their body and then ask if anyone wrote down something that wasn't to do with how their body looks. There are usually a few groans and a sense of being caught out. At one workshop, a female therapist had written down that she liked the fact her body had grown a baby, but except for that one time, the therapists respond in the same way as my clients.

This tells me that we are all prone to thinking about our bodies in terms of our appearance and forget we exist in these incredible instruments. We all have this one body that has been assigned to us. Your body houses you and only you. No one else can reside with you in your body; no one can ever truly know how your body feels to you, or how it responds in different scenarios. We scramble for language to try to communicate an experience to one another, but words only take us so far. Words are the tool of the mind. Your mind may reside in your body, but how connected does your body and mind feel to you?

In order to have a peaceful relationship with food and your body, the mind-body connection needs to be strengthened. If you hate your body, chances are, you're not feeling very connected to it. If you are not feeling connected to your body, you'll have a hard time looking after it and figuring out how to feed it. Your body needs to be your ally in this process, not your enemy.

A mind at war with the body

When you wage a war with your body, when you're frustrated and disappointed with the way it behaves or looks, you push mind and body further apart. The mind effectively says to the body *I reject you, you're not good enough, you're too big/small/short/ugly.* We are not our bodies and yet, at the same time, we are. The chemistry of our body affects the way we think and feel. Our physical state, particularly rest and sustenance, has a big influence over the decisions we make. Take the famous study of judges in Israel, which found the judges' rulings were significantly more lenient at the start of the day and after the lunch break, compared to the harshest judgements that were handed out just before lunch and at the end of the day.

Take a moment to look down at your own body right now. Look at your arms, stomach and legs. Notice what thoughts come up for you when you observe your body. It's unlikely that you look at yourself with an empty mind; you are going to have some thoughts about the shape, size and function of your body. How you talk about yourself to yourself matters. You are inextricably attached to your body whether you like it or not, so wouldn't it feel better to think well of it?

In order to do this, you need to create new beliefs about your body. One of the frustrating parts about making these shifts is that the old beliefs aren't likely to suddenly vanish, especially if they've been around for a long time. So, for a while at least, you'll be holding two different, probably contradictory, ways of looking at your body at the same time. This often means bouncing between the two, embracing the new beliefs one moment and identifying with the old ones the next. Relax. This is supposed to happen. The more you return to how you want to view your body, the less emotionally attached you become to the old belief system.

When it comes to how you view your body, trying to switch to the polar opposite of your current thinking is likely to be a challenge. Going from *I hate my body* to *I love my body* misses out all the stages between love and hate. It's pulling you into the all-or-nothing mindset. When you are trying to introduce a new way of thinking about your body, you want to avoid triggering a mental debate where each side, the old and the new, argue it out with each other. If you do that, the old usually wins because it has had many more years of practice and of gathering cherry-picked evidence to support its view.

To avoid this, we start by softening the old thoughts. There is no point using rational debate to try to convince yourself that how you see your body isn't the truth. Maybe you are fat, but it's not just about what you believe your body is, it's the meaning you then place on that belief. Think about a part of your body that you don't like and then ask yourself *So what?*

I hate my thighs. So what?

My stomach is too big. So what?

I'm fat. So what?

Instead of trying to see your body differently, let's begin with changing the meaning you are making about its perceived flaws. You think the meaning is actually a fact, rather than something you have constructed, believed and then treated as an indisputable truth.

If you believe your body is too big and you make this mean that no one would ever find you attractive, imagine how that's going to affect your behaviour. Confidence is attractive. The belief that no one would find you attractive means you will behave like someone who expects this to be true. How likely are you to go on dates or initiate sex with a partner if you believe others find you hideous? If you are single, you are going to avoid the situations that would increase the chances of finding a partner. Time will slip by and if you haven't found a partner, you'll use this as evidence that no one does, or will, ever find you attractive.

One of the easiest methods you can use to soften current beliefs is to use qualifiers. This just means that whenever you catch yourself having a stressful thought about your body, you add a *but* to the end and then qualify the statement with something more positive. This could look something like this:

- *I'm so ugly...**but** I have people in my life who love me.*
- *I hate my double chin...**but** my hair is thick and shiny.*
- *People must be disgusted by me...**but** I got that promotion last week.*
- *Urgh, look at my jelly belly...**but** my body brought life into the world.*
- *I've gained weight...**but** I'm going to try not to catastrophise.*
- *I look awful in that photo...**but** I did have a great time that night.*
- *I'm useless, I binged again...**but** I am still trying to figure this stuff out.*
- *My stomach is massive and bloated...**but** my body is working hard for me.*
- *I hate myself...**but** I'm willing to learn how to feel better about myself.*

The problem is not just bad body image per se; it's the fact that how you see your body has become so entwined with your self-worth. You don't have to love all the parts of your body to find some respect for it; you just need to stop wishing so strongly for it to be different. This is your body today. When you want something so desperately, perspective flies out the window, along with balance and nuance. This then decreases the chances of you getting what you want.

You assume that in order to like your body, you need to mould it into a more acceptable shape. You think changing your body will change the way you see it. I'm proposing that body image goes much deeper than that; you need to change the way you see it first. Try accepting your body for just a few seconds. You don't have to like it right now, but could you, for a moment, stop struggling against how it looks and feels today?

The practice of gratitude

Gratitude is fast becoming a bit of a trendy word in the self-help industry. I deliberately didn't mention it at the beginning of this chapter because I have found some people have an interesting reaction to it. I had a client who struggled with the word because he could recall, when he was a child, always being scolded for being ungrateful and told he should be more grateful. Gratitude had such a negative connotation for him because it was something he was supposed to express to placate the adults around him. In our work, we changed the word grateful to thankful and then he was able to work with it.

Gratitude and appreciation are so important in body image work because they shift our perspective. I've had so many people insist that they must be terribly vain and shallow because why else would they have become so fixated on what's wrong with their appearance? This is not about vanity, it's about pain. The pain of not feeling good enough. It begins with a few thoughts about your appearance that create painful feelings of separateness and fear. The feelings cause the mind to pay close attention to those thoughts and assign importance to them. The thoughts escalate the feelings and the feelings escalate the thoughts.

We are programmed to move away from pain, but the more attention and energy that becomes invested in the idea that our body isn't good enough, the bigger the problem becomes. For some, those first seeds of *there's something wrong with me* get planted at a very young age. As our identity and self-image develops, new beliefs, like the branches of a tree, grow and spread, but they all emerge from the same damaged roots.

When I talk about gratitude, I am not telling you that you should be grateful, but if you are willing to give it a go, the potential benefits are enormous. Gratitude is an attitude and a practice, as well as an emotion, and has been shown to have extraordinary effects on the body. Research at the HeartMath Institute found that just five minutes of gratitude practice regulates heart functioning, which in turn balances the nervous system and improves emotional self-regulation. You can actually measure the impact gratitude has on heart function. The heart beats in a more coherent rhythm and this state of heart coherence can last for a few hours after the gratitude practice has ended. This means that gratitude is not only good for the mind, but it also has a measurable and lasting positive impact on the body.

This is one of the reasons health is always more than what you're eating. When people beat themselves up about their food choices, they don't feel good and those feelings have an enormous impact on health. Emotions like anxiety, dread and disappointment all reduce heart coherence. Even if you aren't experiencing a racing or pounding heart, your heart rhythm becomes more erratic when you are feeling these unpleasant emotions. Our emotions have a direct impact on the heart. There are more signals going from the heart to the brain than from the brain to the heart, and this may be why when we feel something to be true in our hearts, rational scrutiny alone usually isn't powerful enough to change the belief. We become invested in our beliefs at the heart level, so this is why we need to shift our emotional state if we want to change the way we see something. Our brains won't believe it until we feel it.

If you feel like you have very little to be thankful for when it comes to your body, that's okay – you're not used to looking for things to appreciate about it. To get started, you can't beat a good old gratitude list. It may feel like hard work to begin with, doing anything new often is, but it's a very powerful exercise.

Just before we go to sleep and just after we wake up, our brain waves are slower and longer, which means we are at our most suggestible at these times. Before you go to sleep and when you wake up, write down five things to be thankful for about your body. Ten things a day might sound like a big number, especially if you're trying to find new things each day, but if you try to be specific, according to what happened that day, there will always be new things to draw on. When you struggle to find the specific, then go broader and more general. Here are some ideas to get you started:

Specific	General
That Sunday lunch was delicious.	My body works tirelessly for me.
I enjoyed sex with my partner today.	My eyes can see.
I strolled to the park.	My ears can hear.
I cuddled my pet.	I have good skin.
I safely drove to my friend's house.	My legs/arms/etc. are strong.
The sun felt good on my skin.	I can hug those I care about.
I slept really well last night.	My hands can write and type.
Today I had the best ice cream I've ever tasted.	I can walk/run/dance/swim.
	My body breathes for me.
	My liver is constantly cleansing and detoxing me.

While some of these suggestions may work for you, the ones you find for yourself will have the greatest impact. Try to feel that sense of thankfulness, but don't beat up on yourself if you can't. It's natural to have days, or even weeks, where you don't exactly feel your heart swelling with gratitude when you do your list. There may be lots of reasons for that – tiredness, stress, or old thoughts paying you a visit. On these days it will feel like a cognitive exercise, maybe even a pointless one, but consistency is key and so is being willing to do it, even when it doesn't feel like anything is changing. Keep sending your brain off to search for things to appreciate that are related to your body and you'll start to experience a shift in the way you feel about your body. I invite you to commit to doing this for a period of 30 days, and then take some time to reflect and notice what has changed.

You might even feel a bit silly when you identify things that seem, well, a bit obvious, but these are the things the majority of us take for granted. Because they happen day in, day out, it's easy to miss the extraordinariness of the daily mundane work our bodies do.

'There are only two ways to live your life.
One is as though nothing is a miracle.
The other is as though everything is.'
– Albert Einstein

⌘

Chapter 3

Why Control Isn't the Answer to Out-of-Control Eating

'When we try to control, we become controlled;
when we release, we become free.'
– Bryant H McGill

Although weight gain is usually the most distressing consequence of overeating, 'fixing' your weight rarely changes your relationship with food for the better. The results vary, but research shows us again and again that the majority of people who intentionally lose weight gain it back within five years. In fact, many will end up carrying more weight than they did before.

But what about those who don't? Chances are you know someone who has managed to intentionally lose weight and keep it off without seeming to become obsessed with food. These people seem to be telling us that it is possible, so why are so many of us 'failing' at it?

To begin with, there are biological differences at play. Some people's brains may simply be more sensitive to restriction and react more strongly to a perceived lack of food availability. The chain of chemical reactions, which occur when the body loses weight, will vary in intensity from person to person and how this is experienced may be unique to each individual.

Thinking styles and temperament play their part too; we can't help our biology, but our thinking is an area where we can have some influence. This involves taking on new information and being willing to challenge some of our old beliefs. Finding a new perspective creates a calmer internal dynamic. No one makes their best decisions when they are stressed out, frustrated or anxious.

Dieting makes it worse

A diet can be like sticking a plaster over a deep wound. Eventually the plaster is going to become loose and you'll see that the wound was too big so it couldn't heal by itself. It may even have become infected and you're left with an even bigger problem now. Similarly, dieting can be like an infection, which inhibits the process of healing your relationship with food.

If how you eat has become a source of anxiety for you, you'll be confused about what to eat. Because you've freed up the mental energy normally spent stressing over food decisions, you may feel some initial relief at surrendering your free will to the diet rules. New diets can feel amazing; your head feels clear, you feel like you've finally gained control and the numbers on the scale are going down.

Some people who struggle with overeating are really good at diets. When in the diet mindset, it's possible to feel focused and unstoppable. You barely remember how bad you felt when you were bingeing and you promise to remember how good this feels. You believe that if you can just make yourself remember this, you'll never binge again.

However, when you diet, you hand over the decision-making process to the diet, absolving yourself from the responsibility of figuring out what to eat. Going on a diet involves making just one decision – a decision to commit to the diet. Non-diet eating involves making lots of little decisions every day about food. If you are constantly making food choices, which you are later regretting, it's no wonder going on a diet can seem like an appealing idea.

The difficulty with this is that it goes against one of your most basic primal needs – the need to be free. Free to choose what you put into your body and free to have control of your destiny. When you're in a trap of compulsive eating, a diet does feel a lot like freedom at the beginning, but you'll soon find it's just a different trap. At some point, the rules of the diet become stifling, so you start negotiating with them. Sometimes it's the odd exception that gradually becomes more frequent; other times you simply launch yourself from the diet wagon straight into a full-on binge.

My client Emma was good at following the rules of a well-known weight-loss programme. To begin with, it was fun and she was delighted with her weight loss. 'There was a time when I was logging my weight every week. I don't know whether I just decided not to anymore, but sometimes I would not comply very well points-wise. I wouldn't want to log in on the Friday and so I didn't. I gradually stopped doing it because, in my mind, I knew how to do it, but without the structure of recording points, I drifted away from it and fell back into old patterns again. Finally it became that I hadn't done it in so long. I was conscious of regaining the weight to a degree. I remember thinking *I've lost it before so I can lose it again.* It wasn't as hard as I thought it was going to be.' But what Emma found was that once she had relaxed the rules, she wasn't able to put them back again. It was as if her brain just wouldn't let her, in spite of her repeated, yet futile, attempts to get back on the diet wagon.

Once your brain knows how to undermine your control, it's very difficult to restrict again. This is why I believe dieting can be dangerous. It can create a disordered relationship with food where there wasn't one before. This is especially true for children and teenagers – these are such important developmental years; their bodies and brains are growing so fast. The younger someone is when their relationship with food and their body gets messed up, the more deeply ingrained and distorted their view of their bodies can become.

However, people can and do develop problems with food later in life. My client Bethany had always had a pretty relaxed relationship with food and a good body image. When she was 35 she had a baby and, for the first time in her life, she decided to diet to lose around 8lbs of post-pregnancy weight. 'For the first time I learned about calories so I simply tried to eat less of them,' she said, shaking her head. 'I would be really "good" for a couple of days and then the next few days I would go on these massive sugar benders. At one point I managed to lose quite a bit of weight, but then I started to get really anxious about what I was eating. I was paranoid that the calories listed on packaging weren't accurate and I started weighing myself several times a day. I would binge and restrict, feeling fat one day and okay the next. I know my weight wasn't changing that much, but it really felt like it was.'

Once you learn the calorie content of food, you can't simply forget that information. Dieting changes the way you see food and often, the way you see yourself too. Food becomes something to be burned and earned. When you have been relying on sums to figure out what your body should be allowed to consume, it's hard to remember that there was once a time when eating was a carefree event. For some of you, that may have been a very long time ago.

The bigger picture

I remember my mother dieting only once in my life. I was probably about ten years old when she lost around two stone (30lbs) by following a Rosemary Conley exercise programme and eating a calorie-controlled diet. Afterwards, she seemed to eat a bit more consciously, but appeared to have an okay relationship with food and her weight stayed the same for the rest of her life.

As she was losing her battle with cancer, she was sitting in the bath one day and gazing down at her wasting body. Her flesh had fallen away rapidly over the last couple of months. Her once-strong legs were now feeble and thin. 'I had always wanted a gap between my thighs,' she told me wistfully, tracing her fingers down the inside of her legs. 'But I never imagined I'd end up paying this price to have one.'

This was such an important moment for me and, with her words, my mother imparted a wonderful gift. Chasing weight loss as a means to happiness is futile and be careful what you wish for. Sometimes, or even usually, it just isn't worth it. Many people have admitted to me that, at some point, they have longed to get ill. Not life-threateningly so, but ill enough to have weight loss enforced on them. I can remember thinking that way too, so I can understand it if you are having these thoughts as well.

You may have been holding on to the belief that if you just got to your ideal weight, you'd feel great about yourself and all desire to overeat would vanish. Really think about this for a moment. Think about what overeating looks like in your life. Is that really going to transform by itself? In your heart of hearts, do you think that managing to sculpt your body into a particular shape will mean you never have to struggle with overeating again?

As an exercise, I often ask my clients how old they would like to be when they die, assuming their health was okay until the end. This question feels like it comes out of the blue, so it usually catches them off guard. I often get suspicious looks; they're not quite sure where I'm going with it. Some are more resistant to answering than others; a lot of us feel uncomfortable if we think about our mortality.

Try this exercise for yourself. If you could pick an age to live to, what would it be? When you have your number, just hold that number in your mind. Now, let's fast forward over the next few years and imagine you are now the age you picked out. You are lying on your deathbed and the end of your life is drawing near. When you look back over the last however many years, what would you like to see to feel like your life was worthwhile?

I encourage you to pause and sit with this question. The first things that pop into your head show you what your core values are. If you want to know what's important, really important, to you this exercise can show you this.

I've yet to meet anyone, even someone struggling to function due to an eating disorder, say anything about weight or body shape. The top ones that come up the most are about relationships and having some sort of impact or influence on the world. I think of these as love and purpose. That's what most people want from their life. Other answers include travelling the world, being successful at work, being a good person, and other more specific goals like writing a book or running a marathon.

I can be a pretty good procrastinator, but give me a deadline and some external accountability and it's a safe bet that I'll meet it. Death is the ultimate deadline – Dead. Line. I sometimes wonder if I knew that I was never going to die whether I would actually do anything. I honestly don't know.

When so much energy is being thrown into battling your weight, it may be that your values are being misdirected towards something that will not, and cannot, give you what you want. You may believe that losing weight means being more attractive, which then means that people will think more highly of you.

Trust me, I see conventionally beautiful people in my practice and, in their day-to-day lives, more often than not, they find themselves the subject of people's instant dislike. People tend to like people based on how they feel when they're with them. If someone is attentive and makes us laugh, we're probably going to like them. If someone is beautiful and we feel unattractive by comparison, those pangs of insecurity are going to make us less likely to feel positively towards them.

Steve grew up as a heavier kid. He was bullied relentlessly at school and, at 14 years old, he was so consumed by self-hatred that he was contemplating suicide. At 16 years old he contracted meningitis and was very ill for several months; during which time he drastically lost weight. He returned to school and the response was extraordinary.

'People who had never given me the time of day were suddenly interested in me,' he said. 'These girls who were so horrible to me a few months before now wanted to sleep with me. I was so confused. I did sleep with them, but I hated them for it and I hated myself even more for doing it.' Steve went on to become a bodybuilder and fitness coach, but still struggles with food and body image. A day of bingeing will be followed by not eating anything at all for a few days. When he looks in the mirror, the person looking back at him is 'obese' (his word, not mine). He can't see the definition in his abs and he seeks out constant reassurance and feedback from others about his appearance because his own eyes continue to deceive him. His self-esteem is so low because he cannot trust that anyone really cares about him. Any positive regard feels conditional, based on him looking a certain way. He says, 'I live my life in terror. Terror of being that fat kid again. The one that no one liked.'

What do you imagine would be different in your life if food wasn't an issue and if your body looked the way you wanted it to? You may believe you'd feel different and people would treat you better, but you would still be you. Many of your thoughts would still be there. So much of your thinking has become automatic because it has been repeated so much. You would have the same fears and insecurities as before and, even if some people treated you differently, be careful what you wish for. Conditional regard can feel inauthentic and unsatisfying. What about the you who stays the same, despite your changing body? Is it only your outward appearance that makes you worthy?

My perceived lack of control over myself and my unhappiness with my body was a convenient scapegoat for everything that wasn't going well in my life. For several years, my binge eating was *the* problem in my life; the one area where I felt like I just couldn't get it together. It grew so big. I was convinced that when I solved it, life would be wonderful and easy. If I could get control of this, I imagined I would be able to do anything.

Time and time again, when people exercise tight control over their eating, the result is food obsession. Take it from a therapist who works up close with anorexia (the most extreme form of food control) – it is not possible to significantly restrict your food and not become obsessed. We are designed to eat and when we mess with that system too much, it will come at a great cost.

You don't need to go as far as developing anorexia to experience this psychologically and biologically driven food obsession. Kelly did a liquid diet for nine months. She lost a lot of weight fast, putting her in the 'healthy' range, according to her BMI. She was in a bigger body before embarking on the very low calorie diet (VLCD), which was recommend by a dietitian and she was monitored by her GP during the process.

She says, 'The physical hunger disappeared early on. I wasn't hungry anymore, but I started to become really obsessed with food. I started to dream about food. I used to watch cookery programmes every evening and just devour them like I was actually eating.' After hitting her goal weight, she resumed eating and her appetite felt insatiable. She felt completely out of control, quickly regaining all the weight she had lost. It took her a long time to heal from the experience and make peace with food and her body.

Culture pressure and dieting

There is a growing movement, somewhat ironically driven by social media, which aims to dismantle diet culture. The message to people is that it's okay to not be trying to lose weight all the time; it's okay to exist in a bigger body and we need to stop moralising food as good or bad, it's just food. Diet culture is everywhere. In fact, it is so imbedded in our day-to-day life that you may not have even noticed it.

- Diet culture is justifying dessert because you've been 'good' today.
- Diet culture is calling yourself 'naughty' for having a second helping.
- Diet culture is accepting guilt as a normal response to eating a particular food or skipping exercise.
- Diet culture is preaching healthism (the idea that we have a moral duty to prioritise physical health above all).
- Diet culture is the lack of 'normal' shaped bodies in the media.
- Diet culture is believing weight loss equals health and that your value as a person is significantly impacted by your weight and shape.
- Diet culture is moralising food choices as good or bad.
- Diet culture is praising weight loss as an impressive accomplishment.

You may think these things are just part of normal, everyday life. They are! And that's the problem. Once your eyes have been opened to diet culture there is no closing them again. This can feel quite jarring as you start noticing those around you engaging in subtle (and not so subtle!) diet talk. This will take some careful navigation on your part; you can't stifle their free speech and most people won't respond favourably to being told they can't talk about something in front of you, but you do have control over how you protect yourself and side step these conversations.

Adopting a non-diet way of eating doesn't mean you throw away all structure around food. Structure and routine will be your friend as you try to make changes to the way you eat. Reducing the number and variation of food decisions you have to make every day might help you, especially at the start of your journey. For example, finding a staple breakfast that satisfies you and keeps you going means that's one less food decision you have to think about.

Being non-diet in your approach to food is about resisting external pressures about what and how much to eat. It's about rejecting the idea your body should look a certain way and deciding you no longer want to believe you are a better or worse person based on the way you eat.

I often say to my clients, 'I don't care what you eat. I care about why you eat it and whether you are happy with your reasons.' You get to decide what reasons sit well with you. If you change the way you make your food decisions, so that they align with your values, then you can eat in a way that serves you on all levels – physical nourishment, emotional needs, the desire for pleasure and connection, and to experience satisfaction. The last one is so important and often not given the attention it deserves. Feeling satisfied with what you eat is going to be your path to mental freedom around food. Feeling satisfied will help to stave off feelings of deprivation, which will in turn reduce reactive bingeing.

Let's say you are at a big celebratory event on a Saturday night and there is cake. The cake is beautiful to look at and it's your favourite type of cake (I'd probably go with lemon or banana, but you go with your favourite). You eat a slice and it's perfect; it's sweet and soft and delicious. You finish your piece and there is plenty of cake left. You think for a moment; do you want another slice? It really was the best cake you'd ever tasted and you'll probably not get the chance to have it again. Some of your friends are going in for a second slice and you decide to enjoy another one too. You feel a bit stuffed and caked-out, but you still maintain it was the nicest cake you've ever eaten.

Now let's switch to a different Saturday night. No party tonight. Instead, you're home alone, so you eat two slices of whatever cake is available because you're feeling bored, sad and tired.

Consider the difference; in both scenarios you ate two slices of cake on a Saturday night. In neither situation was the decision you made objectively good or bad, but the reasons were very different. Chances are, you are going to feel differently in each situation about what was, in effect, the same behaviour – eating two slices of cake. I use this example to illustrate that it isn't about focusing on what you eat, but understanding the reasons behind your food choices. Doing this from a curious and calm place will help you start to make some sense of what could be driving your overeating.

Food as a relationship

Whenever I'm at a social event with new people, if the subject of what I do for a living comes out, inevitably at some point, someone will pull me aside to tell me about their difficult relationship with food. This has probably led me to a somewhat biased view that a lot of us are, at least, a little bit messed up when it comes to food and body image.

Everybody has some kind of relationship with food. We have to interact with food every day, several times a day, and we put the food inside us. That's a pretty intimate relationship. You weren't born with the knowledge that what and how much you ate would impact the size and composition of your body. At some point in your life you would have learned this information. I wonder how this information came to be realised for you. Perhaps it was a remark linking greediness to being fat, or you saw your mother trying to restrict her food intake to lose weight. At what stage of life did you learn that how much you moved your body affected how fast you burned the energy in your food?

Understanding how your relationship with food and your body developed will not automatically fix the problem, but it is the beginning of changing how you understand your difficult relationship with food today. We need to look at this with a new mind if we are going to find a different way. Einstein said, 'we cannot change our problems by using the same thinking that created them.' Your repeated efforts to change have left you tired and battle weary. Perhaps it's time to stop and take stock before figuring out what to do next.

The reason for a self-compassionate approach is to create a calmer state from which to gather some perspective. Heightened emotional states affect our thinking. If a thought and feeling align, that becomes the indisputable truth to you in that moment.

Think of a time when you were really angry with someone you care about for something they did (or didn't) do. While you were angry your brain would have flooded with angry thoughts about that person; angry thoughts you believed wholeheartedly while you were mad at them. When your anger subsided, those angry thoughts either vanished, or became mere shadows of what they were, as your view of that person became more favourable again.

As humans we seem to have adopted this terrible habit of believing what we think. If we're having a thought, we assume it must be true. After all, why else would we be thinking it? It's a bit grandiose when you stop to consider all the millions of contradicting thoughts and opinions there are out there and we believe that somehow, we must have the right ones. It can be scary or liberating to let go of believing we know everything. It all comes back to perspective.

The truth is how you think about your life will determine your day-to-day actions. Same with eating. How you think about your problem is a big part of how it shows up. Changing how you think about food may be challenging, but it is possible. I hope this book can be a guide for you. We will certainly be looking at what is getting in the way and how you can go about clearing the blocks. You may not agree with everything you read in this book; it may even be better if you don't simply swallow everything I'm saying whole. I encourage you to engage your own critical thinking and figure out what parts are most helpful to you. Take what you need, discard what you don't.

In part two I will explain how you can use the RALIC method to help you break free from the cycle of overeating. You will probably experience a lot of confusion in this process. This is okay; it may even be desirable. Confusion occurs because new information is competing with old information. If you catastrophise feeling confused, you'll escalate the feeling from confusion to frustration and this will make you want to throw up your arms and go running back to the old familiar ways.

Controlling from fear

One of the most frustrating things about compulsive eating is that it doesn't seem to make sense. You know it has become harmful to your wellbeing and self-esteem, but you can't seem to get a handle on it. You try to make sense of why you keep doing it and sadly, many people end up deciding it must mean there is something terribly wrong with them; that they must be a defective, weak-willed person who keeps failing to fix themselves. It may seem natural to conclude that the answer should be to try harder. Just do better tomorrow, just stop eating this or that, just go to the gym, join a slimming club. Whatever you do, don't stop fighting until you gain your control back. Control or be controlled, that's the motto.

Particularly if you are someone who binge eats, you swing between being in and out of control with food. It's one or the other, no middle ground, and you may believe the answer is to find a way to stay in control. Newton's third law of motion states that every action has an equal and opposite reaction. If you are trying to tightly control your eating, that pendulum is going to swing back the other way at some point and you are going to feel out of control again.

Trying to control something or someone is often a fear-based response, a way of managing uncomfortable feelings of anxiety and uncertainty. When we feel unsafe, when life feels scary and unpredictable, a common response is to look for things to control. When we are in control we feel like masters of our own destiny. However, life is unpredictable, things happen that we cannot prevent. We can argue against this as much as we want; we can try to prepare for every eventuality, but we will exhaust ourselves in the process and things still won't turn out the way we wanted them to. Needing to control involves a lack of trust in our ability to handle the unexpected, which increases anxiety, further heightening the need to exert control.

Writing this book became something of a battle for me. At one point I had to scrap three months' worth of work and start all over again. This was devastating at the time. I battled with not feeling good enough. I struggled with imposter syndrome (*who the hell do I think am, writing a book?*) and with wanting to control the flow of inspiration. This led to feelings of panic and an inability to write anything.

Early on, I decided to get away by myself for a couple of days. I rented a tiny gypsy hut in a small village in the English countryside. There was no TV or Wi-Fi, not even a shower. On arrival I found it was even smaller than I imagined and I suddenly had this sense of feeling very alone. Even though I was in the countryside, it felt cramped and small compared to London. I felt tears coming; I just wanted to go home. Several times in those first few hours I contemplated jumping into my car and fleeing back to the familiarity of my cosy flat. I longed for the noise and distractions of the city. What was the point of staying if I was feeling like this? I certainly wouldn't be able to write in this state.

I must have sat on the bed (which pretty much took up the whole hut) doing nothing for two hours, just fighting with my mind and shedding a few tears. I felt like leaving would be a sign of failure, but what was the point of being here if I wasn't using the time to write? Finally, I surrendered. I surrendered because I was exhausted from fighting with my mind and I didn't know what else to do. I surrendered my idea of what these two days should look like – I'd had images of me sitting by the fire pit, pen in hand, channelling my inspiration and writing a book that would cure the world of compulsive eating. The hut was in an orchard with apples, plums and raspberries that guests were free to pick and eat. I saw myself living off the land, taking breaks to do yoga and go for strolls in the countryside while dictating brilliant and insightful ideas into my phone, which I would later write into this book. The reality of being there was very different to how I had imagined it and my heart swelled with disappointment; mainly disappointment about how I was reacting to the situation, more so than the situation itself.

When I let go, I accepted that maybe I wouldn't write a word. Maybe this experience would be something different to what I had planned. Maybe it wasn't about being productive and smashing out an impressive word count. Once I accepted this possibility, I felt peaceful and calm. I stayed with this sense of calmness for a while, and then I opened my laptop and started to write.

Battle the bulge, battle yourself

Compulsive eating is about control, whether it's feeling like you have it or you don't. To the compulsive overeater, control is highly regarded as the most desirable thing (after weight loss). In relationships, if someone tries to control the other, they will end up either destroying the relationship or maintaining a very dysfunctional one. Dysfunctional relationships are very unsatisfying because they do not provide the sense of connection and safety we need.

Again, it's the same with food. We have an interactive relationship so, if you become the controlling partner with food, it's no wonder that you end up feeling disconnected and unsatisfied. The longer you have been fighting with food and your weight, the stronger the opposition has become. It knows all your weak spots and how to exploit them. Because the fight is inside you, you are your own opponent. You may feel like you are fighting something on the outside, but the battle is an internal one. Food is a neutral object until you imbue it with meaning and turn it into a powerful enemy.

If your eating struggle has been going on for years, you are in an all-out war. The best outcome of a war is for both sides to agree to surrender and make a peace agreement; each side agreeing not to seek domination over the other. When the war ends, a time of growth and rebuilding follows; this is an opportunity to welcome in some peacetime and start building something new.

⌘

Chapter 4

Not What to Eat but How to Eat

'Pull up a chair. Take a taste. Come join us.
Life is so endlessly delicious.'
– Ruth Reichl

There is a new kind of diet that is taking off these days – it's called the *high fact* diet. We have so much information about nutrition, maybe too much. Never before have we known more about nutrition and biology and yet, I suspect, never have we been more confused about what we are supposed to eat. Being confused about what to eat isn't much fun, but it is a privilege. We can recognise our privilege without feeling ashamed about it. For most of us, we have never gone hungry because food wasn't available or we were too poor to buy it. Today overeating is able to thrive in this land of plenty we inhabit. We possess a very strong drive to eat; this is a biological necessity in times of scarcity, but we don't live in those times anymore.

You may believe you have a pretty good idea of what you are supposed to be eating. When I ask clients to walk me through what a 'good' day of eating looks like, I get to see how they believe they should be eating. Almost invariably it isn't enough food! They think they should be existing on protein and vegetables, or that they should be staying under a certain number of calories, but considering how different and complex our bodies are, how are we ever supposed to know what the right amount of food is? Guidelines are just that, a guideline. We spend so much mental energy trying to work out what, when and how much to eat, that, with so much conflicting information out there, it's no wonder we're all confused about what to put on our plates.

The humble calorie

Let's look briefly at one of the most widely accepted nutrition guidelines: caloric intake. In the UK, the NHS recommends a maximum limit of 2,500kcals for men and 2,000kcals for women each day. If you are confused about how much you should be eating, often calorie counting can seem like the simplest and most straightforward way to try to manage your food consumption.

As you may already know, all food is made up of three macronutrients. They are carbohydrates, proteins and fats. The current accepted caloric value of these macronutrients is 1g of carbohydrate = 4kcal, 1g of protein = 4kcal and 1g of fat = 9kcal. You may know your numbers, but do you know what a calorie actually is?

Calories are units of energy. One calorie is the amount of energy it takes to raise the temperature of one gram of water by one degree Celsius. Does that sound like a lot or not very much to you? For most of us, it's hard to imagine what this really means. To calculate the calorie content of a food, a method called bomb calorimetry is used, which involves burning food to see how much heat it releases. This is then measured and these measurements give us the calorie content of that particular food.

The bomb calorimetry method assumes our bodies are behaving like furnaces on a fixed thermostat. The calorie calculations do take into account that we pass some calories in faecal matter, but it does not offer the flexibility to take into account the variability of absorption rates from person to person. With two people of a similar age and size, one may have a much higher caloric requirement than the other, even if they are less physically active. This may be because their body doesn't absorb the same number of calories from the same food, as well as other metabolic variations.

If you prescribe yourself a fixed limit to your daily allowance of food, you don't take into account your body's varying energy needs, which fluctuate from day to day. If you are logging your food and exercise, you may 'allow' yourself to eat more food on the days you exercise, compared to the days you don't – because you've 'earned' it. You use external information to try to figure out what your body needs. However, we have inbuilt regulators, which we need to learn to hear better, and they are called hunger and fullness. Some people feel hungrier on days they exercise, but others don't. Many people report feeling hungrier the day after exercise, rather than on the day itself. This could be down to the body doing its reparative work. If you are keeping your food intake within a prescribed calorie limit, decided by setting food on fire, you are not trusting your body to signal what it needs. You may find yourself more preoccupied with food, or undercutting your requirements, and this increases the risk of bingeing.

If you are looking outside of yourself to try to figure out what your body needs, you'll bump up against all the contradicting advice out there. Should you be doing paleo, keto, plant-based or intermittent fasting? Promoters of particular dietary approaches can be very evangelical about their opinions and have turned the way they eat into their vocation. It's become their job and identity. I choose to believe that many of these people are very genuine and truly believe their way is the best way, but they make a mistake if they assume their way will work for everyone. For those who feel confined and trapped by food rules, or who don't have the time or inclination to turn their nutrition into a full-time occupation or regime, these messages about the 'best' way to eat can be frustrating. For some of us, finding the time and energy to plan and prep, and manage constant thoughts about food can come at a considerable cost to our overall wellbeing. This may be you if you feel pressured to follow a particular way of eating.

Intuition and eating

This book is about becoming free from overeating, and by overeating, I mean, of course, problematic overeating. If you think you are never supposed to overeat, or that overeating is a terrible crime, then any time you eat more than you think you should, you are going to feel bad about it. This is how a disordered relationship with food develops. To free yourself from problematic overeating, you'll need to be able to discern between the universal experience of eating more than you physically need in the moment and overeating in a way that has a long-term detrimental effect on your overall wellbeing.

If you weren't overeating, what would your day-to-day interactions with food look like? It's worth spending some time considering this question. Without the vaguest notion of what normal eating is for you, how will you know which direction to head in? You want to change, but it's important to know what you want to create, as opposed to only focusing on what you are trying to get rid of. You want to stop your overeating and for this, you need a new way of eating that isn't a diet.

So what's the answer? Research indicates that perhaps the best solution to improve your relationship with food is to follow the principles of intuitive eating, as devised by two nutritionists – Evelyn Tribole and Elyse Resch. They came up with the principles after seeing first-hand how even so-called 'sensible' dieting (making health-based choices and allowing 'treats' in moderation) kept resulting in rebound weight gain among their clients. The intuitive eating approach recognises that our relationship to food and our body needs to change in order to break free from unhelpful cycles of problematic eating. I cannot recommend more highly that you check out their book *Intuitive Eating* to appreciate the method in full and understand the evidence behind it. Intuitive eating is living by principles, rather than rules, when it comes to how you eat. The ten principles of intuitive eating are:

1. Reject the diet mentality
2. Honour your hunger
3. Make peace with food
4. Challenge the food police
5. Respect your fullness
6. Discover the satisfaction factor

7. Honour your feelings without using food

8. Respect your body

9. Exercise – feel the difference

10. Honour your health – gentle nutrition

1. Rejecting the diet mentality

This obviously involves making a commitment not to diet, but it's more than just that. There are more subtle ways that diet mentality sneaks in. A general belief that you should always be in an energy deficit, because you think you need to lose weight, is diet mentality, as is believing you need to earn certain foods through exercise or cutting back elsewhere, and also categorising food choices as right or wrong and feeling guilty about what you eat.

The diet mentality will try to convince you that you can gain control of your eating by following rules. It will tell you to try one more diet. It will tell you to lose the weight first and then come back to this intuitive eating thing. This doesn't tend to work; you'll end up triggering more last supper eating episodes; you'll become more entrenched in the diet mentality and cause even more psychological chaos around food. If you feel compelled to try another diet, I won't try to stop you. I just ask you to hold in mind the information shared in the previous chapter and come back to intuitive eating when you are ready.

I've never tried cocaine, but I have been told that the first time you do it, you get an incredible high, which you never quite reach again. People become hooked on cocaine by trying to recapture that first high. They still get a buzz, but it is an ever diminishing one compared to the increasing cost to mood, health and their sense of control and choice. Likewise, when someone goes on their first diet, they often do very well (if weight loss is the measure of doing well), but then the weight returns. Each subsequent diet feels harder and harder to maintain. Because they lost weight on that first diet, they continue to pursue the possibility that the answer lies in finding a way to make themselves comply with the diet rules.

Intuitive eating is for people who are tired of chasing the highs and false promises of a diet and they're ready to try something new.

2. Honour your hunger

As we know, food deprivation triggers food obsession and compulsive eating. Compulsive eating is an irresistible urge and also, you can't resist biology. When you ignore hunger, attempt to distract yourself from it, or fill yourself up with low energy foods to try to fool it, there is going to be compensatory eating. This can involve eating much more than you needed to simply make up the energy deficit; your body is getting ready for future famine.

Many people think of hunger as a feeling in their stomach, but it can show its face in many ways, such as light-headedness, feeling cold or having difficulty concentrating. You may also feel physically weaker or irritable. A rise in ghrelin, the hunger hormone, will increase your thoughts about food. Hunger can hijack your thinking and this is one of the reasons why it is so important to treat it with the respect it deserves. One test for hunger is to ask, what food is appealing to you right now? If a wide range of foods are desirable, then the body is probably hungry for food. If you are wanting only one very specific type of food and everything else seems uninteresting to you, you may be wanting something that isn't about physical replenishment.

Let's become willing to befriend our hunger. It's a natural and helpful signal from the body that it's time to eat. It can feel good to experience some hunger before you are about to eat because this is the main need that food has been designed to satisfy, so it makes for a much more rewarding experience to feel some hunger before we eat.

If you have a history of dieting and trying to restrict, it's not advisable to allow yourself to become too hungry as you may be setting yourself up to binge.

3. Make peace with food

You are allowed to choose what you put into your own body. NOBODY gets to make that decision for you. One of the problems with not allowing yourself full permission to eat certain foods is that, by trying to deny those foods, you increase the emotional value of that food. Suddenly, it's not just about the experience of eating the food; the food has taken on meaning about freedom and denial, and this leads to more intense cravings for those foods.

This principle is about giving yourself unconditional permission to eat. Particularly with binge eating, there is often a sense of needing to finish all the food and get rid of it, because once it's gone, you're going to try to be 'good' again. When you truly know that the foods you desire are available whenever you want them, the over-desire for them starts to reduce. The fear is, if you allow yourself to eat whatever you want, you're going to have ice cream for dinner every day. This isn't the reality of it. At first you may find yourself eating all the foods you've always thought of as bad or forbidden, but when you give yourself permission, fully and unconditionally, the way you feel about those foods starts to shift. This is often the scariest principle, but push through it and there is freedom waiting for you on the other side.

4. Challenge the food police

The food police live inside your head. They have made laws about eating, which have been taken on from outside sources. They tell you what you should or shouldn't be eating. These rules have become etched into the law books of your mind, available for you to beat yourself about the head with every time you fear you have committed a misdemeanour.

Many people describe a feeling of freedom and release when they go on a food binge. It can feel like being out of prison on day release (I imagine!), but it's a temporary and fleeting taste of freedom. You escape to overeat and you overeat to escape. It's one of the reasons almost everyone who overeats distracts themselves while they do it, usually with things like television, phones, internet or magazines. It's a way of quieting down the law enforcers who would otherwise be telling you what a terrible person you are for eating this way.

That inability to put the half-eaten packet of biscuits back in the cupboard or return an unfinished tub of ice cream to the freezer is partly down to the role of the food police. If you think those foods are bad, you will believe they need to be banished and you end up punishing yourself by stuffing away food you don't even want anymore.

5. Respect your fullness

This is not to be confused with the hunger-fullness diet, neither is it a rule about stopping the moment you're full, but you'll need to become willing to pay some attention to your fullness levels. This may sound straightforward, but so much eating is done unconsciously and on autopilot. When we're unconscious about our eating, we don't use our body's signals in the decision-making process. Eating ends when the food is gone, regardless of whether we were feeling full ten minutes ago.

You may experience eating to the point of being physically uncomfortable, even in pain, and yet you still feel driven to keep eating. It will only be possible to respect your fullness if you know you have full permission to eat what you want, when you want it (see principle 3). If you know you can eat it whenever you want, you don't need to worry about getting rid of it now. You don't have to worry about being hungry later because if you are, you can eat again. When there's no impending deprivation looming on the horizon, it's much easier to listen to what your body is telling you in the moment. Your appetite is no longer being driven by the anxious anticipation of what future food decisions you will be making.

6. Discover the satisfaction factor

I think this one is my favourite. If you aim to eat in a way that prioritises satisfaction, you win on so many levels. The focus is on enjoying what you eat and eating what you enjoy; doesn't that sound appealing? When in a compulsive cycle with food, you'll rarely be enjoying the food itself. You're not even conscious of eating it most of the time.

Eating has been designed to be a rewarding activity and satisfaction is the ultimate reward. We chase satisfaction in everything from our careers to our relationships; it really is the holy grail of life. A disordered relationship with food will block eating satisfaction at every turn. You chastise yourself, *'How dare you seek satisfaction when you should be seeking moderation?!'* But satisfaction has a moderating effect. If you eat a meal and end it feeling full and sated, you are less likely to be thinking about food over the next few hours – as long as you're not anticipating deprivation, of course.

Ask yourself what you really want to eat. When you consider a food choice in your mind, check in with your body and see how that food choice feels. When you do eat it, savour the food and pay attention. Notice the smells, the taste and how you feel. Seeing your food disappear into your body will increase satiety signals. This is why it's so much easier to overeat when you are distracting yourself and not paying attention to your food.

There will be various foods you associate with overeating. Eating these foods mindfully and with full permission will give you a very different experience to eating them in your usual out-of-control way. It will be an opportunity to notice how your body responds to the food and it strengthens the mind/body connection. Paying attention in this way helps your brain to make associations with how different foods make you feel. This will help you get in touch with your internal cues, which is another step towards self-regulated eating.

7. Honour your feelings without using food

For some people, this will be the hardest principle to live by, especially if you have been regularly using food to cope with some very difficult situations in your life. Eating often makes us feel a little better, so we may choose to eat for this reason, regardless of whether we feel hungry or not. Using food as a soothing mechanism is not a crime; it's a common response for many people. When babies and small children are upset, food is regularly offered, so it can become a learned behaviour. It becomes problematic when it's the main way of dealing with your emotions, or when the eating itself is now having a detrimental effect on your wellbeing.

Learning how to recognise and manage your feelings without using food may mean making significant changes in other areas of your life that have nothing to do with food. Many people who use food to cope with emotions have become afraid of their feelings. Just as you can develop a better relationship with food, you can also improve the relationship you have with your emotions. It's not uncommon to catastrophise uncomfortable feelings and believe that if you're feeling bad, something must be horribly wrong. You may experience an urgency to get rid of uncomfortable feelings.

This means, like with eating, there is a tendency to want to control how you feel, but trying to control your feelings, a bit like eating, can lead to feeling detached from your emotions one moment (in control) and overwhelmed by them the next (out of control). Chronic emotional eating develops when food becomes the main way to manage your feelings.

To varying degrees, how we feel will always influence our eating. Even hunger is a feeling in the body. How we feel is such an important part of the puzzle when we are figuring out our overeating. We will keep coming back to this throughout this book because it is such an important part of the picture.

8. Respect your body

Body respect does not mean you have to love the way your body looks, but it will involve neutralising some of the critical thoughts you have about why your body isn't good enough. It's about accepting that you *have* a body and that this is the body you have today. It works very hard for you, striving to maintain physical homeostasis and allowing you to touch, feel and exist in this world. Your intention, though it may fluctuate, is to recognise your body as worthy of respect and deserving to be cared for.

It may feel as though your negative feelings towards your body are ingrained into the very fibre of your being. If so, it can feel like a mammoth task to address your body image. There are some exercises and resources at the back of this book that may help you. Exercises work because improving body image is a practice. You have practised feeling bad about your body for such a long time that seeing your body this way is effortless. The goal is to shift how you think about your body first and this will shift how you feel about your body. You want to feel better before you change your beliefs, but this is the wrong way around. To begin with, all you need is a willingness to feel better in your body now, as it looks and feels today.

9. Exercise – feel the difference

The all-or-nothing mindset will tell you to either do a proper workout or what's the point? In your mind, going around the block for a 15 minute walk requires greater effort than the perceived pay-off, but it's the compound effect of small efforts that really make the difference. For most people, a 15 minute walk would cover more than a kilometre each day. That's 7km a week, 30km a month or eight and a half marathons a year!

Exercise for you may be synonymous with weight loss and either burning off or earning food. Generally, I tend to move away from the word 'exercise' for this very reason; it tends to be attached to reward and penance and has become another thing you feel like you should be doing more of.

We used to be told we should be doing cardio to burn off our fat. Now it's all about strength training. You're told to increase your muscle mass so that you increase your metabolism and that's the best way to burn fat these days. Never mind that both cardio and strength training cause an increase in hunger signals as the body seeks to redress the energy deficit. You're just expected to ignore that part!

That said, the body likes to move. We have these bodies to navigate us through the physical world. When we move, increased circulation improves oxygen and nutrient delivery around the body; our hearts become stronger and the brain releases endorphins, which improves our mood. Movement has so many physical and mental benefits, which, overall, increases your energy levels.

Intuitive eating means finding your joyful movement. No punishing gym routines or personal training sessions, unless you really do enjoy that. Start small, a short daily walk while listening to a podcast if that appeals to you, and don't under-estimate how great ten minutes of stretching before bedtime can feel.

10. Honour your health – gentle nutrition

BE GENTLE!! Sorry to shout, but some people freak out when told that one of the principles is to prioritise nutrition; they'll say to me, 'But you said intuitive eating was about not having rules and eating what I wanted. If I have to focus on nutrition, isn't that a contradiction?' No, it isn't and there is a reason why it's the last principle.

We live in a culture of healthism, which can create an attitude of shaming those who don't appear to be prioritising their physical health. Mental health comes first; it always starts with the mind. Create a healthy mindset first and then, from that mindset, you'll be in a better place to make decisions that feel good for you and honour your health.

Finding the middle ground

When it comes to disordered eating, most people will fall into two categories. In the first group are those who believe they know exactly what they should be eating and they just want help sticking to it. The second group believe they don't know what they are supposed to eat; they feel very confused and they want someone to tell them what and how much food they should be consuming.

Whichever group you relate to, the answer is always the same – *intuitive eating*. Whether it's difficult for you to relax the rules or it's a struggle to create structure, these principles will help you do either or both. They are the middle ground between control and chaos. You think you need to be doing the opposite of what you are currently doing, but often that's simply the other side of the same coin.

In recent years, intuitive eating has been hijacked by the diet culture brigade and touted as a tool to lose weight. Intuitive eating is not about weight loss; it is about creating a healthy relationship with food and your body. Some people do lose weight through learning to eat intuitively, but if weight loss is the goal it will interfere with your ability to give yourself full permission to eat, and the diet mentality will keep derailing your efforts.

The most common reason that people struggle to implement intuitive eating is usually because the focus on weight loss has sneaked back in. The desire to lose weight has been with you for a long time, so please don't make it mean you've failed if the desire keeps returning – just notice it, let it go again and reset your intention. The RALIC method you'll be learning about in part two can help you with this process.

There is no pass or fail when it comes to intuitive eating, which is great, but it also means it is down to your subjective opinion when it comes to deciding how well you think you are progressing. If you are very self-critical, your self-assessment of how it's going may not be fair. If you are used to rules, you may struggle with not having numbers to reassure you that you are making progress.

Using numbers by which to measure yourself fuels black-and-white thinking so, by being willing to feel the discomfort of not having hard evidence, you'll start seeing the grey. You'll find the middle ground that is so essential to breaking free from chaotic eating. If it were a seesaw with 'in control' on one end and 'out of control' on the other, you'd be sitting in the middle, safe and secure, away from the sweeping highs and crashing lows.

⌘

Chapter 5

An Inward Journey

'It takes courage...to endure the sharp pains of self-discovery rather than choose to take the dull pain of unconsciousness that would last the rest of our lives.'
– Marianne Williamson

The more I discover about myself, the more painfully conscious I am of being far more complicated than my mind may ever be capable of understanding. My journey is a never-ending one. When I accept that there is no end point, no destination where I can say I've finally made it, only then can I relax and enjoy the journey. The journey of self-awareness will include difficult climbs, magnificent views, boring stretches of the same thing and even toilet stops, which is where you let some of your sh*t go.

Me, myself and I

How well do you really know yourself? Try thinking of three words that you would use to describe you. Lots of people find this difficult; some only manage to find one or two words. Finding the language to convey who we are can be hard.

Language limits us, but it's the best tool we have when it comes to understanding ourselves, making sense of who we are and figuring out our place in this world. When you have identified your three words, ask someone close to you to tell you which three words they would use to describe you. Were any of them the same words you chose? Were they even in the same ballpark?

There are three parts that combine together to build a picture of who we think we are and where we fit in the world. They are:

1. How we see ourselves.
2. How we think others see us.
3. How others actually see us (and how/if this is communicated to us).

As the great RuPaul always says at the end of his show, 'If you can't love yourself, how the hell are you gonna love someone else?! Can I get an "amen"?' No RuPaul, you can't. You can still love others when you don't love yourself. However, your ability to experience intimacy and connection will be diminished; that doesn't mean you aren't capable of love though. If you are full of self-loathing, it will be hard for you to feel loved. Even if people deeply care about you, you'll have a hard time believing it. You may still generously give love if you don't like yourself, but you'll struggle when it comes to receiving it back.

If how we see ourselves is very different to how others see us, we can be left with a deep, existential angst that makes us feel disconnected from people and from life. This is what I see when I read about famous people who are adored by the public, but deeply unhappy. Take the much loved Robin Williams. People found him kind, funny and warm, and yet I imagine that he saw himself very differently. We need to reconcile our inner and outer worlds to feel grounded in who we are. If these worlds are too far apart, it's hard to find a place to belong.

If you want to know yourself better, look at how you are reacting to those around you. The people in our lives, especially the ones we find the most difficult, can be brilliant teachers to those of us who are willing to learn. The way you respond to what is going on outside of you is always a reflection of what's going on within.

Let's say you and I went for a coffee with a third person, who neither of us had met before. I'm going to call this non-gender-specific person, Sam. Sam is funny and entertaining, with lots of interesting anecdotes. At least, this is what I see. Perhaps you find Sam arrogant, domineering and not interested in anything we have to say. We both saw the same person and witnessed exactly the same behaviour. Objectively, Sam is neither funny and warm, nor arrogant and domineering. These are just our subjective impressions and how we form our impressions of others can give us clues about what is going on inside us.

We see the things outside of us that resonate with the things inside of us. What is your history with arrogance and domination? You may have been dominated in the past and the experience left you hypersensitive to noticing domineering traits in others. Or you may have an unacknowledged part of you that desires to be the dominator, because it means you are in control, and being in control gives you a sense of safety and protection.

If you don't go within and get interested about your own responses to the people in your life, you'll miss wonderful opportunities to understand something about yourself. If you are holding on to an image of the kind of person you believe you should be, or were told you should be, you are going to be incredibly judgemental and critical towards the parts of yourself that don't live up to that image. That kind of self-criticism provokes shame, and shame is the biggest block to increasing self-awareness.

How we shame ourselves

I didn't develop binge eating disorder until I was 25 years old. For me, it developed quickly and seemingly out of the blue. I had never struggled with food and weight before, but it became all consuming. My appetite was voracious and out of control and I gained weight quickly. When my partner at the time started to notice something was wrong, I broke down. I tried to explain what was going on and how out of control and scared I was. His response, which I will never forget, was to look at me puzzled and say, 'But I thought you were stronger than this.'

With those words, I felt the cold blade of shame slice through my chest and for a moment, I didn't breathe. I felt like a complete failure and utterly alone. *I thought you were stronger than this.* His words weren't spoken with malice, he was genuinely confused. My behaviour had changed so fast and this new version of me did not fit with the image he had of me in his mind.

For years his words tormented me and made me ache every time I remembered them. I resented him for not understanding, even though I was expecting he should understand something that I could not. I can't pinpoint the moment it changed, but slowly I came to the realisation that most of the time, we shame ourselves. *I* was the one who made it mean I was weak and a failure. *I* used his words to reaffirm what I already believed. It was *me* who thought my behaviour was out of character and it was *me* who couldn't reconcile my eating problem with the way I wanted to see myself. This wasn't about him. I would rather feel shame and resentment about what he said to me, than look at the way I was speaking to myself. This was a big part of what kept me stuck for so long.

Guilt is a response to believing you've done something wrong; shame is a response to believing you are what's wrong. Shame is an isolating experience, a deep sense of separateness and worthlessness. As Brene Brown puts it, 'Shame erodes the very part of us that believes we are capable of change.' Shame also stops us from wanting to know ourselves, causing us to hide those shameful parts from the gaze of others and thereby perpetuating the belief that there is something wrong with us.

In babies we see the core emotions like joy, sadness and fear, but what about shame? It seems that we learn how to feel shame later in the game of life. To feel shame, we need to be cognitively developed enough to judge ourselves. Our self-judgement often arises through what we perceive others are thinking, like with my ex. It was my perception that he thought I must be weak and failing at life, but this wasn't what he said. I added layers of meaning to what I now believe was simply his bewilderment at the sudden changes in me. It's not whether people are thinking critically about you that matters; what matters is what you believe about it.

When you were growing up, if one of your parents told you that your body was too fat, or that you were greedy, you would have believed it. You would have felt shame that there was something 'wrong' with you. Or perhaps your parents never directed their judgements at you, but they placed a high value on their own appearance. In this case, you would have witnessed this and learned from their example that it is your appearance that makes you worthy, and comparison to others is the only way to measure your worthiness.

Most people I meet feel very ashamed about their overeating. You may believe something is wrong with you. Maybe you have achieved what you wanted in other areas of your life, but when it comes to food, you feel like you are failing and it doesn't seem to make any sense. There is a lot of pressure in our current climate to exercise restraint in our eating patterns and to look like we are taking care of our health. If we are in a 'normal-sized' body (that is, one that society deems to be acceptable), we are saved from dealing with assumptions from others about our health and behaviour. If you struggle with overeating and you are in a bigger body, it can be especially tough, because it may feel as though your pain is being exposed for the whole world to see.

Amy lived in a bigger body and wasn't happy about it. When she lost a lot of weight, her colleagues' attitudes towards her transformed. Suddenly she was the subject of admiration and compliments. One colleague commented that she looked great compared to the 'monster' she had been before. She was horrified that this was how he had seen her. When she regained the weight, she couldn't get that comment out of her head.

During meetings she would imagine him thinking how she had become a 'monster' again.

Shame blocks change

Are you angry with yourself for your overeating? If so, are you willing to forgive yourself? Notice, I didn't ask if you could forgive yourself, only if you are willing, because that's where it starts. It involves turning inward and giving yourself a break from the self-shaming. Personally, I don't believe there is anything to forgive, but many people hold very strong views about just how wrong they believe their behaviour to be.

Using others can be an amazing way to work through shame; it's one of the reasons why I run therapy groups for binge eating. When you see someone else going through the same thing as you and you hear them being so harsh to themselves about it, it's much easier to feel compassion for them than it is for yourself. Group members act like a mirror for each other; you see yourself in others in a way that isn't tainted by your unrealistic expectations and your personal history of perceived failure.

We have to deal with shame if we want to break free from overeating. Again, this is why making a commitment to finding self-compassion is so crucial. Without it you'll keep triggering the shame response. Imagine teaching something to a six-year-old and every time the child makes a mistake, you tell them they are useless and a failure. You tell them they should be trying harder, but that they're never going to be able to do it anyway. How teachable do you think that child is going to be? Stress plus shame will block learning and growth – every time.

Releasing shame isn't about adopting a Pollyanna-like positive attitude. There will be disappointments along the way and it will be important to acknowledge them as such. You are probably going to overeat again and feel like you've messed up. Often, the first place to implement a change is in how you respond to your overeating, not the overeating itself – that usually happens later. First we need to change the emotional energy around the event of overeating itself. Up to this point you have been trying to fix this by resolving to fight harder and that often makes it worse.

Later on, we will look at how to use the RALIC method as a tool for releasing you from inner conflict, so you can make a different choice, but self-awareness will be crucial for you to be able to put it into practice. Both individual and group therapy are very good at helping you to understand yourself better, but there are lots of ideas and concepts already out there that can help. Becoming more self-aware means building a clearer picture of some of your traits and tendencies that may currently be working for you, or against you, when it comes to food.

Permitters and restrictors

Broadly speaking, people who struggle with disordered eating fall into one of two camps – the permitters and the restrictors. This is a concept first introduced by Geneen Roth in her book *Women, Food and God*. Simply put, restrictors have a hard time giving themselves the freedom to eat certain foods and permitters struggle to choose *not* to eat certain foods. The outcome is the same – food obsession and misery. Both restrictors and permitters feel out of control, so the restrictors tighten the reins in terror and the permitters rebel through fear of being caged and starved.

Also, and this is a broad generalisation based on my own observations, restrictors often see their bodies as bigger than they are. Sometimes, but not always, permitters go the other way and see their bodies as smaller than other people might. We see this in those magazine weight-loss stories where someone undergoes a dramatic physical transformation, which was triggered by a photo where they saw that their body looked bigger than they had realised.

There is a big difference between how these two groups are perceived in our diet-obsessed culture. The behaviour of the restrictors is celebrated and applauded. They are, after all, doing what they are supposed to do – exercising restraint and making 'healthy' choices. This societal reinforcement adds to their fears about what might happen if they were not restricting or being hypervigilant about what they ate. The permitters, on the other hand, tend to be subjected to society's fat-phobic attitudes and judged harshly for their apparent lack of control. This confirms how many of them see themselves – as people who cannot manage their desire for food.

Where they are the same is that they are both controlled by food and fear; the restrictors by the fear of allowing themselves to eat what they want, and the permitters by the fear of not being allowed to eat what they want. Each of them has their self-worth tied up in how they eat and the shape of their body. They both reside in their own type of prison.

Sometimes the restrictor breaks out, binges and then rushes back to lock themselves in their cage, feeling annoyed for believing they could be trusted and reaffirming to themselves that they can't. The permitter will sometimes try to impose rules or start a diet to contain their overeating, only to smash their way out of self-confinement when they feel claustrophobic and trapped.

No one who has a disordered relationship with food truly gives themselves permission to eat – even the permitters; their eating is at least partly driven by a belief in some future restriction and if they were really giving themselves full and unconditional permission to eat, it wouldn't be followed by feelings of guilt. Remember, guilt comes when you believe you have done something wrong.

If you identify as a permitter, perhaps the past has shown you that any attempts to forcibly reduce your food intake is futile. The rebellious part of you that resists being controlled is powerful. Your challenge is to develop some structure around your eating in a way that lets you feel like you are making a choice. Many permitters struggle with boundaries in relationships. They find it hard to say no to people and this extends to themselves as well. At some point in their lives, they learned that saying no was not allowed, or something that only selfish people do.

Have you heard the saying, 'the way you do one thing is the way you do everything'? Well, this is never truer than with your relationship with food. Sometimes it's easier to make changes in other areas of your life first, before you try to change your eating. It can be easier to start somewhere else because there is less resistance and a lower emotional response. Many people find that some shifts start to happen with food when they challenge the way they are functioning in other areas of their life.

If you are someone who struggles to say no, practise. Find somewhere in your life where you often say yes, but tend to feel a bit resentful afterwards. You may think you just like saying yes to people, but are you saying yes because you can't say no? Saying no is going to feel weird and wrong to you, and if you feel unable to do it, then be curious about what you believe it means to say no. You may need to challenge some old beliefs and see how saying no can be an act of self-kindness in some situations.

Figuring out if you are a permitter or restrictor is one step towards greater self-understanding. You may know immediately if you are a permitter or restrictor, but this doesn't have to be a binary concept. Many people swing between the two, so you might see yourself as half and half, or perhaps 80% permitter and 20% restrictor. The permitter/restrictor concept is helpful in its ability to simplify how we are approaching food and control in our lives.

The four tendencies

Let's take this self-understanding a little further by looking at Gretchen Ruben's four tendencies. This was not designed specifically for eating, but rather, it's about how we meet expectations. Ruben's four tendencies are: the Obligers, the Questioners, the Upholders and the Rebels. To figure out which one fits you best, think about what holds you accountable when it comes to getting stuff done. Are you someone who is affected by external expectations, such as other people counting on you or an impending deadline? Or are you someone who makes their own rules and takes pride in being self-accountable? You may also be someone who responds well to both inner and outer expectations, or someone who rejects all expectations.

Obligers	Upholds outer expectations, resists inner ones
Questioners	Upholds inner expectations, resists outer ones
Upholders	Upholds inner and outer expectations
Rebels	Resists inner and outer expectations

I see more Obligers in my practice than any other tendency. They are the traditional 'people pleasers', able to keep promises they make to others, but they struggle with being accountable when it's only for themselves. The Obliger's challenge is to learn to put themselves first when appropriate. If they can turn themselves into someone they want to please, meeting their own expectations may become a whole lot easier for them.

Laura, a recovering Obliger, put it this way, 'Looking back I have noticed that if there was no external governance, I would just keep eating. Up until I went to university, I naturally had some imposed structure on my meal times, but once I was on my own in my first year at uni, that's when my eating ramped up. Later on I shared a student flat and I was eating with others, so it calmed down a bit. Diets acted as an external governor for a while, but at some point you realise it really is just you and the diet. No one will know if you "cheat".'

If you are an Obliger, it's very important to you to be seen as a good person and the way you have learned to do this is by being obliging. Putting yourself first may seem like a selfish act to you, but I'm talking about making yourself enough of a priority to be able to practise better self-care. Self-care is about replenishing yourself and restoring your resources, which will make you better able to perform your role as the caretaker anyway. Put your oxygen mask on first before helping others with theirs.

Questioners resist any outside pressure to do, be or act in a certain way. They need lots of information about what is expected of them and why. Only if it makes sense to them will they comply. They are internally accountable and almost impervious to peer pressure. I don't meet many Questioners in my work. My guess is that they are more resistant to diet culture than the average person, so they are less susceptible to feeling pressured to change their body. Perhaps this is why so few of them develop a disordered relationship with food, or it could be that they are less willing to seek help from external sources.

For many, the Upholder seems to be the most enviable tendency to possess. They are excellent at meeting their inner expectations, as well as outer ones. On the outside they appear to be conscientious and get a lot done. They make excellent employees and tend to be reliable, but what happens to the Upholder when the outer expectation conflicts with their inner one? This is when they have a problem on their hands. Being an Upholder can be anxiety provoking because you may attempt to juggle all expectations. You'll often find yourself in no-win situations, especially with the conflict between the outer pressure to control food and the inner pressure exerted by a body that wants to be fed.

The challenge for the Upholder is to become aware of how they are internalising outside pressures. As an Upholder, it would benefit you to be mindful about what external messages you expose yourself to. Upholders and Obligers are the most likely to be triggered by what they see and hear.

Andrew was the ultimate Upholder and he found it very uncomfortable not to follow the rules. 'When I read in a fitness magazine that that we should be eating fewer than 40g of net carbs every day, I couldn't get that number out of my head. I logged my food and my macros meticulously and would feel so guilty if I went even slightly over at, say, 45 grams. Yes, it sounds absurd, but I really could beat myself up over 5 grams! That's like a teaspoon!'

And last but not least, we have the Rebel. The Rebel rejects all expectations. Whether the expectations come from the outside world or within themselves, it makes no difference to them. Expectations from others and even their own expectations can feel stifling to the Rebel. They are particularly sensitive to not feeling free; they'll perceive attempts to trap them that aren't really there. Rebels need to be particularly kind to themselves on their journey to creating a better relationship with food, as they can feel easily frustrated with the process. They need to learn that giving up control is not the same as being controlled, but this needs to be discovered and experienced for themselves; they probably won't take my word for it! The ideas in part two will be particularly helpful to the Rebel as they focus on feeling free and making choices.

Knowing which of the four tendencies fits you best will help you to build up your awareness of your inner world so you can start putting together how you may be perpetuating your struggle with eating. It's not about trying to forcibly change your tendency, but rather, understanding how to work with it, so you can derive the benefits and manage the costs.

Judge less, understand more

As you gain more insight into yourself, there will be some self-judgement arising. Once you realise something about yourself that you don't believe is helpful, it can be tempting to say to yourself *Right! I'm just going to stop doing that!* The difficulty is, a lot of the time, insight by itself isn't enough to get rid of the long-established patterns of behaviour, but what you can do is start by using these insights to play out your usual patterns with an awareness of what you're doing. Something starts to shift the moment we become the watchers of ourselves.

In order to be able to apply the RALIC method, a certain level of self-understanding is crucial. Recognising the flow of thoughts and feelings, seeing how they move and evolve through your experience of overeating, is a necessary step to making changes. This means you have to pay attention. We can't make new choices or do something different without bringing our attention to it. If you find this stressful and your thought processes don't seem rational, don't worry, you are in good company here. This isn't a rational problem – our relationship with food is rooted in our emotions and the beliefs we formed long ago.

If you are ready to open your eyes to face the obstacles in your mind, try this – just stop overeating; just make yourself stop doing it. What happened when you read that sentence? Your mind may have already begun to protest. What did it say? Just notice, and hold those judgements in check, otherwise you'll spin yourself away from the potential to increase self-awareness.

I'm not saying you can just stop overeating; I know that's not how it works, but you can discover a lot if you try to stop it and be willing to notice what that experience is like for you. It's not about whether you manage to do it; it's about deliberately provoking the part of you that doesn't want to give up overeating, so that you can increase your understanding of it. It's about being willing to come face-to-face with the part you prefer to keep hidden and the part you have so much judgement, or even loathing, towards. If you can stop and listen to this part of you, you may learn something new about yourself and about why you overeat.

When you have mastered the ability to watch your destructive patterns without becoming as emotionally triggered as you were before, and when you can observe your compulsive eating without shaming yourself for it, you will dampen the inner conflict. It won't vanish; it's still there, but it hasn't completely taken over your mind. This is the first step to liberation.

⌘

Chapter 6

Who We Are (and Why it Matters)

'We know what we are, but not what we may be.'
– William Shakespeare

Little kids are adorably gullible, aren't they? Wonderful little sponges ready to unquestioningly soak up any information given to them. As a child, whether you were told 'Father Christmas is real', 'we're nearly there', or 'the dog went to live on a farm', you believed it. You trusted the messages that the adults passed on to you.

As you developed in age and reflective capacity, many of your beliefs got updated. Your growing brain could change and adapt to new concepts, switching direction in light of new information. This process slows with age, but it never disappears as long as you still have some sanity left. You can find evidence for this in your life if you look for it. For example, what about when you changed your opinion of someone because you heard about something they'd said or done? Or when you eventually admitted that your partner may have had a point once you had calmed down after an argument?

If you weren't able to change your thoughts, your thinking would simply grind to a halt after the first thought you had about anything. Nothing could evolve, and you would stay the same, frozen in time.

Old thoughts may never die

Your oldest beliefs will have the deepest roots, stored in the complicated neural networks firing in your brain. Your beliefs comprise many interconnected thoughts, like a web, so dismantling them would be a complex operation. The solution is to find ways to loosen the hardwiring of the old neural networks and build new circuits. New thoughts actually change your brain! Just reading this book will require new neural pathways to grow, in order to consider these ideas.

One of the reasons why change might feel uncomfortable is because you will be holding the old and the new in your brain at the same time. This feels like you are living in a contradiction as the old thoughts and new thoughts compete for your attention. One day you believe one thing to be true, and another day the opposite feels true. This is common when it comes to releasing the idea of intentional weight loss. Some days the old thoughts come back and all you want to do is figure out what you need in order to stick to a diet. It may be that the old thoughts never completely leave you; they might just retreat into the shadows, ready to spring forth if you so much as look in their direction. This can make people nervous about inadvertently triggering old patterns. In part two I am going to talk about how to disrupt this process.

Identifying with thought

The way you were treated growing up has had a big impact on your self-image today. You grew up saturated in the beliefs and attitudes of those around you. As a child you saw your family as representatives of the wider world. How you were treated sets up expectations for how the world will treat you. What parents deem to be important in life are strong messages to a growing child; little eyes are always watching.

You may have been told that your body was wrong in some way, or scolded for your food choices, but even if you weren't, you will have witnessed the relationship your parents had to food and their own bodies. Even if you never had an unkind word directed towards you about your own relationship with food and body, if they were struggling themselves, you received the message that weight gain is bad and food restraint is good – this is the foundation for disordered eating.

Listen to your self-talk and notice where you place yourself within it. Listen to the difference between **You** *mustn't eat that* and *I mustn't eat that*, or **You** *should stop after one* and *I should stop after one*. If you hate what you see in the mirror, do you think **You** *look awful* or *I look* awful?

I hear people jumping between the first and second person constantly when they talk about this stuff. If you say *you* a lot, chances are these were never your original thoughts, but adopted from other people, whether that's family or diet culture. Either way, it's not you. Try changing your *you's* to *I's* and notice how it feels different.

Your identity is made up of how you see yourself, how you feel about yourself and how you view your place in the world.

If you were to only take one thing from this book, it's this – understand that the way you view yourself needs to change before you will be able to make consistent changes in your behaviour around food. This is important because if you view yourself as someone who struggles with food, your struggles have become part of your identity. As long as you continue to see yourself as someone who is out of control with food, you'll keep returning to the same old patterns that support this image, especially during times of stress or overwhelm.

During my struggle to stop bingeing I would do quite well for a couple of weeks (by this I mean I would find a peaceful place with food and be practising the intuitive eating principles), but all it would take was a bad day, or feeling run down, to derail me. Before I knew it I would be back in the cycle again, unable to pull myself out of it, no matter how hard I tried to get back on track. Today I don't see myself as someone who binges after a bad day. I can feel stressed or depressed and an old thought of eating on it may arise. I look at this thought and think *That's not me anymore*; I just don't identify as someone who does that.

Notice that little voice in your head, the one that's constantly narrating your life, reminding you of the past and using this to predict your future. This voice tells us who we were, who we are and who we are going to be and we build an identity on this information. Identity statements tend to start with I AM. So you may think, *I am* greedy or *I am* never going to be able to sort out my eating. These identity statements are part of the mental picture you hold of yourself. Some of your I AM statements shift and change naturally throughout your life and even throughout your day, e.g. *I am* tired or *I am annoyed with this weather*.

Pay attention to the language you use. Are you more likely to say, 'I *feel* stressed' or 'I *am* stressed'? The first one implies you are having an experience and the latter suggests you are the experience. This may sound like I'm being pedantic, but the way you speak to yourself matters. These small shifts in language can loosen the well-worn neural networks and interrupt automatic thinking.

I wonder what your particular I AMs are when it comes to your relationship with food and your body image? Have a look at some of the ones I hear the most and see if any of them resonate with you.

'I am fat.'

'I am disgusting.'

'I am a failure.'

'I am weak-willed and undisciplined.'

'I am out of control.'

'I am never going to be able to change.'

When you think these things often enough they start to feel like facts, but feelings aren't facts. Similarly, beliefs aren't facts either; they are just our thoughts. It's the emotions that accompany the thoughts that make those statements above so sticky. When you have a thought that invokes a strong feeling, your brain assigns special importance to the thought. Your brain thinks that because there is a strong emotional reaction, you'd better pay extra attention to it, so you keep thinking it and it becomes truer and truer for you. Thoughts that don't have an emotional attachment tend to come and go, easily forgotten.

Let's look at the statement, 'I am fat.' This may be an emotionally charged statement for you that evokes fear, anxiety, disgust or shame, but there is a whole body positive community who are seeking to reclaim the word fat and reduce the negative connotations and assumptions surrounding it. Someone in the body positive community may say, 'I am fat' and experience feelings of defiance and pride. The emotional response to a thought always comes down to what you are making it mean, not the thought itself. The meaning may have been learned many years ago, when you believed everything you were told, but you get to decide whether to reinforce your meaning, or challenge it by looking for a new perspective.

To change a belief it'll be easier if you soften the old one first, just as you might loosen the earth around a weed before pulling it out. Softening identity beliefs involves making smaller shifts in thinking, like replacing *I am never going to be able to change* with *I am still learning and willing to try something different.* It's not realistic to convince yourself something isn't true by going to the hard opposite. *I am fat* probably won't switch to *I am not fat* very easily. You won't believe it, so you'd be better off moving towards a thought like *I have fat, but I am not my fat*, or *I am fat, but that doesn't mean much about my worth as a person.* Look for information that will support your new fledgling thoughts, so if you want to believe that being fat isn't the end of the world, start following fat-positive accounts on social media, or think about people you care about who are fat – does their weight make you care about them any less?

Search for anything that may confirm the belief you want to instil. Back to the Shakespeare quote from chapter two, 'The eye sees all, but the mind shows us what we want to see.' You think you are observing life as it is, but we are each constructing our own version of the world. How else could it be that we can watch the same film, or read the same book, yet come to very different conclusions about the characters and story?

Finding self-compassion

Let's say you've just binged. Again. The old self-berating thought-tapes play; *I'm useless, I can't believe I did that again, I've failed, I'm fat.* Rather than trying to disentangle all the thoughts and coming up with new ones, ask yourself a question. When you ask a good question your brain has to search for information to provide an answer and this interrupts the usual, well-worn narrative.

The statement 'I can't believe I did that again' is so interesting. Notice there are two *I's* in that statement; the 'I' who can't believe it and the 'I' who did that again. This belief highlights how the inner conflict works. It's a splitting process – one part of you is upset and frustrated with the other part. Later on in the book we will look at how we can utilise this process to our advantage.

A question you could ask yourself is *What is the kindest interpretation of this moment*? If it's hard for you to imagine what that could be, consider what you might say to someone else in the same position as you. Would you say, 'You're useless, I can't believe you did that again, you've failed, you're fat'? Of course not. It's not okay to speak to people that way, but that also means it's not okay to speak to yourself like that either. The kinder interpretation may go something like *Yes, I am feeling disappointed that I binged again. Something is going on for me that I'm struggling to understand. I may be confused about what that is right now, but I am trying to understand myself better.*

Defending our beliefs

How you think about things really does matter. Your body responds to your thinking and your thinking responds to your body. If you have an angry thought, your body responds by creating angry chemicals, which fuel more angry thoughts, which fuel more chemicals. If your body is depressed due to a physical deficiency of some sort, this will trigger depressed thoughts. Life may start to lose meaning and this will increase the biochemistry of your depression. Body and mind create a loop, each egging the other on until it becomes an established pattern, or until you, or something outside of you, interrupts it.

We all think, prioritise and process things very differently from one another and this is easy to forget. We are so convinced that people must be thinking in a more similar way to us than they actually are. It's why others' behaviour can be so frustrating sometimes – we put ourselves in their position and imagine what *we* would be thinking in order to behave like that and then we project that back onto the person. Person A will think *I would never forget their birthday, so what does it mean that they forgot mine? Oh, it must mean they don't care about me because if they cared, they would've remembered. I care and I always remember.* It could be that Person B doesn't view birthdays as a big deal. They may be one of those people who actively avoid a fuss on their own birthday, so they can't understand why Person A is so upset. Person B thinks *They seem really upset over a birthday present. It's just a present. Why are they being so materialistic? I treated them to lunch the other week and I worked my butt off helping them move house last month. They are being so unreasonable. How can they accuse me of not caring?*

We live in a world of presumptions, misunderstandings and poor communication. We rarely stop to ask people what they are thinking, choosing to mind-read instead.

So many people I meet are very secretive about the extent of their misery around their overeating. If this is you, those close to you may have a bit of an idea that something is going on, but because they don't have the full picture, they are filling in the gaps based on what they imagine must be going on. They are never going to get it right. This leads you to feel judged and misunderstood by those closest to you, and increases your sense of isolation and separateness.

We can get very defensive when it comes to what we believe. Just look at how people defend their opinions when it comes to topical debates. Everyone believes their opinion to be the right one and that's what most beliefs are – opinions. Imagine how much more inclined you are to protect a belief, or rather *an opinion*, that you have held for many years. Look to your parents; you'll have very strong opinions about what they did right and wrong in the way they raised you. You'll have formed these opinions as you were growing up and they probably haven't been properly scrutinised for a long time. You may already be feeling uncomfortable about my insistence at calling them *opinions*. What if I told you that you were completely wrong in your assessment of their parenting skills? Can you take a moment to be with the possibility that your opinions about what they did right and wrong are not true?

Notice your resistance. Notice where you feel it so you can recognise it and learn to tolerate it without jumping straight to dismissal. You will feel resistance in the process of changing your relationship with food and it's important to recognise what that feeling is when it arises. It will be accompanied by defensive thoughts, but can you notice them without latching onto them? Relax. You are not going to lose something important, even though it may feel like it – there is nothing to defend. This is just your ego trying to protect opinions that have been integrated into your identity. What if revisiting some of your old opinions could make you feel better? Would you rather be right or would you rather be happy?

One person, many parts

I hated the part of me that compulsively ate. I wanted to get rid of it permanently and my quest for a long time involved searching for a way to do that. Accepting that I could not remove this part of me was a tough pill to swallow at the time. I only managed to get to the point of no longer wanting to rip away parts of myself because it was hurting too much to try.

The struggle with overeating is an interaction between different parts of you. Getting to know those parts intimately, without trying to destroy them, will ultimately lead you to freedom. This is almost impossible to do when your thinking is clouded by heightened emotions such as shame and guilt, so we need to find a way to shift how we feel, as well as how we see ourselves, in order to change.

You may wish to view yourself as a cohesive, consistent person, but the reality is that we are more like chameleons, shifting and adapting to the situation and environment. Rather than being one thing or another, it can be helpful to think of yourself as being made up of parts. There is a kind part, a selfish part, a silly part, a serious part, plus 100 more seemingly contradicting parts. There is a part of you that wants to overeat and a part of you that doesn't. Your current circumstances may activate one part over another. Just binged? The part that doesn't want to overeat anymore rises up in frustration towards the part that succumbed to the binge again.

Who will you be if you are no longer someone who struggles with food? This was the big question Kate was grappling with when she wanted to overcome her overeating. By her mid-thirties she had three Masters degrees under her belt, as well as a successful career and stable marriage, but food was her daily struggle. Food, and particularly her weight, had felt like her Achilles heel since her teens. She had grown weary of the battle; she realised something needed to change in a way that would be permanent, but she didn't know what that was.

Kate's story

'I was tired of eating, but what was the alternative? It meant I had to be able to sit with myself in those hours normally taken up with food and eating. What am I supposed to do in that time? Hours of time in my head, with my thoughts. Was I okay with that? What would I be thinking about instead?

I was listening to a lot of podcasts at this time with people talking about their "truth" and asking the listeners, what is your truth and what is your identity? There was a lot of identity/truth talk. What did that even mean? I couldn't articulate my truth and maybe that was the problem. I kept feeling like I was supposed to be writing something, or I was supposed to be giving something to the world; maybe start my own podcast, that kind of thing. I had these thoughts and ideas, but maybe because I didn't know what my truth was, I didn't feel like I was contributing enough to the world.

I had picked up Eckhart Tolle's book *A New Earth* some months previously, but when I started it, I'd thought *Woah, I'm not ready for this* so I put it down, fully intending to revisit it in the future. A few months later, I decided to give it another go. I was listening to the audiobook while cutting through the graveyard near my home. There was this chapter about identity and Eckhart was saying that when people tell him they don't know who they are, he says, "congratulations!" People would look at him like he was crazy and he'd say to them, "the only problem with not knowing who you are is if you think you should."

I think my response to this went something like *Whhhaaaaat?* This was a totally new perspective. I stopped and immediately replayed the whole chapter again, trying to soak in the message. I remember thinking something important was unfolding. The truth of those words resonated with me so deeply, my life changed forever in that moment. I knew them to be my truth. After much searching, I finally found something that felt true to me.

I started doing these walking meditations. The idea is that you're walking along, looking around and simply noticing. You only use first generation words to describe what you're seeing. You don't use any adjectives, so you'll be walking along saying things like "tree", "path", "bench" rather than describing what you see by imposing meaning on everything.

Soon after Eckhart Tolle had dropped his identity bomb on me, I was doing my walking meditation on a grey, drizzly morning. *Flower...Pigeon...* I cut into the Embankment gardens, *Gate...Tree...Disney princess... Wait, what?* I stopped and stared. A few yards away were this mother and daughter. She was a tiny little three-year-old in a Disney princess dress with a pink and silver tiara on her head.

As I watched her, it all came together in my mind; the morning scene between mother and daughter as they were getting ready for their day out. In my head I saw the conversation they must've had about going out in that outfit and it looked something like this...

Mother: What do you want to wear today honey?

Little Girl: (gleefully) Disney princess!

Mother: (looking doubtful) Really? Disney princess? It's kinda raining out there.

Little Girl: Disney princess!

Mother: Are you sure? Maybe some jeans or something?

Little Girl: (insistently) No. Disney princess! And I want my wand and my tiara please.

Mother: (sighing) Alright. Disney princess then.

I saw the whole conversation playing out in my head and watched the little girl get her way that morning. She got to be a Disney princess today. Now here she was, walking around in this totally inappropriate outfit for the weather and location. The bottom of the dress was dragging in the mud and the chiffon was becoming all tatty, but she was oblivious to it all, waving her wand around, twirling and laughing.

I thought to myself *Trying to define who you are is a childlike endeavour. Who am I? Who are you? Because right now you're Disney princess and tomorrow you will be not-Disney-princess.* It's just so naive and childish to think that we have to be one thing forever. Today is Disney princess and tomorrow will be something else. You can be whatever you want to be at the time and it doesn't define you as a person. You don't have to have a constant truth and identity, but perhaps, just for today, my truth is Disney princess. Rock on.

This thought blew my brain, but I thought *I'm good with this, my truth is that I don't know who I am and I'm okay with that.* It wasn't even that it was okay, it was actually preferred. As Eckhart Tolle would've said, "Congratulations!" I just got it; I saw myself in a way I hadn't before and something deep inside me was unlocked. I felt a release from needing to prove anything, to myself or anyone else. There was this big question I had been grappling with for so long – *Am I okay with who I am now?* In that moment, the answer was a resounding *Yes.*

To not have to find or construct an identity for myself, to just be whoever I am in the moment – that is the biggest freedom I gave to myself that day. I felt like I lost 75lbs with that thought alone.'

Changing how you see yourself means you need to go inward. It involves a willingness to spend some time with yourself – we can't get to know someone unless we spend time with them. This is no different when it comes to you getting to know you.

For Kate it was about letting go of the person she had always felt she should be. She knew that in order to give up using food as a means of escape, she was going to have to find a way to be with herself during the times she'd normally be overeating. Her walking meditations were her way of carving out time to spend with her thoughts. Walking meditations are a great place to start inner work, especially if you struggle with sitting alone with your thoughts. The bilateral movement of walking activates both the left and right hemispheres of the brain. Your emotional and rational hemispheres are both activated at the same time and they communicate more easily with each other in this state. This is why going for a walk really does clear your head.

Being with me

Going to stay in the hut on my own was a challenging, but ultimately transformative, experience. I'm an extrovert by nature, meaning I get energy from being around people, so the self-imposed isolation threw me into something of an existential crisis where I felt as if I didn't exist. That sounds a bit dramatic, but it made some things very clear to me; namely, that I depend a lot more on positive feedback from others than I have ever felt comfortable admitting to myself. This was a painful realisation, but one I made an effort not to judge myself too much for. I have found that when I accept the parts of me that are messy, needy and vulnerable, the urge to avoid and distract myself dissipates.

By not having access to my usual 'hits' of Netflix, social media and internet, I had no choice but to ride the discomfort of being with me. It was a rough ride at times, but amazingly, what I found on the other side was peace and calm. I came back restored and committed to not flicking on the TV or picking up my phone every time I experienced an urge to distract or if I felt agitated and bored.

This was often the feeling that preceded picking up food for me – an agitated boredom; a sort of restlessness and need for stimulation. Many clients describe a similar experience. What *is* that and how can you learn to manage it without turning to food? Whatever that feeling is, it's a part of your life. Over time you have become conditioned to chase this feeling away with food. Part of undoing this will involve the willingness to experience your feelings. In order to do this, we need to understand what we are making our feelings mean and find a new way to interact with the messy emotional parts of ourselves.

⌘

Chapter 7

Eating to Escape

*'Your pain is the breaking of the shell
that encloses your understanding.'*
– Khalil Gibran

It may be that ALL eating is a form of emotional eating. After all, hunger is a feeling; we say that we feel hungry. Sometimes it starts with bodily sensations such as stomach rumbling, a sense of emptiness or a mild pang. Other times it's a thought, or the sight of food, that causes a shift in our body chemistry. In both cases we interpret how we feel as hungry.

Somebody who does not have a complicated relationship with food will look at the available choices in a cafe or restaurant and base their decision on what they feel like eating. They'll read a menu or look over a display and go with what they feel drawn to; they use very little mental energy when making their selection. This is a very different story for someone who has a complicated history with food. If deciding what to eat is a stressful or anxious experience, you'll find it difficult to make a decision with all that chatter going on in your head. Your inner dialogue may go something like this: *Hmmmm. I wonder what*

I should have. I should probably choose the salad because it's healthier, but that probably won't last me until dinnertime, but then again I am eating out, so I should probably have something small. I could have a sandwich, but I'm trying to stay away from bread, but if I find one of the lower calorie ones, that might be okay. Although it didn't taste very nice last time...

This kind of mental noise makes it hard to check in with your body. If we can't check in with our bodies, we can't *feel* our way to a good choice for us. The exhausting mental battle cuts you off from being able to connect to what your body wants, and this creates feelings of tension, frustration and anxiety. Now you feel bad so you become more likely to reach for foods that have a short-term boosting effect on your mood and these are usually foods that are higher in sugar, salt and fat; foods that you tend to consume with a side order of guilt. There is nothing wrong with choosing to eat these foods, but if you regularly eat them to try to remove discomfort, rather than because you genuinely enjoy them, that's when you may feel like you are being controlled by your cravings.

These days I am very aware of how I feel when it comes to making food choices. The two parts I seek to balance are how I'm feeling now and how I want to feel. If I can, I want to feel better after I have eaten than I did before. I want to feel satisfied. Sometimes this will mean having something sweet and sometimes this will mean resisting. If I am wanting to eat something to escape disappointment, loneliness or my agitated boredom, food won't be able to satisfy me. It would be hard for me to stop eating if I were to start eating from this state.

Over time I have become more skilled at knowing what will satisfy me in the moment. I can't tell you when to say yes and when to say no to food, but I will be showing you how to free yourself to make choices. The sweet spot is learning how to say yes to foods you enjoy for your own good, not saying yes because you can't say no.

The effects of eating on biology

Eating calms anxiety; it's a very effective sedative. Anxiety and stress are biologically connected to fear and threat. They trigger the 'fight or flight' response, causing your sympathetic nervous system to spring into action. Your heart rate goes up and your breathing becomes shallower. Your blood moves away from your stomach and intestines because digestion is no longer a priority. If you were in a life-threatening situation, you wouldn't want to waste energy on digestion as you'd need all the energy you have to run away or fight for your life.

If you regularly live in a high state of stress, you'll be spending a lot of time in the fight-or-flight mode. If you are in this stressed state and you fill your stomach up with food, this signals to your parasympathetic nervous system that the threat is not imminent. The parasympathetic nervous system then calms down the fight-or-flight response; this is often called the 'rest and digest' state. You wouldn't be eating if you were genuinely under attack, so the act of eating is a way of physically reassuring yourself. A full stomach signals your digestive system to start working and this has the benefit of temporarily reducing stress and anxiety at the biological level.

When it comes to depression, the story may be slightly different. We know that sugar and simple carbohydrates increase serotonin levels in the brain and that serotonin has a mood enhancing effect. Eating also stimulates dopamine production, which is linked to reward and pleasure. Dopamine is also linked with motivation and learning and may be a key factor in developing automated behaviours around food.

Food can change how you feel in an instant, and it's available everywhere. Unlike other mood changers, such as alcohol or drugs, it's not something we can abstain from. We imagine that if we can think, then we should be able to make a reasoned decision. However, the more decisions we have to make, the more the quality of those decisions start to deteriorate. This is known as decision fatigue; we get tired because our mental energy is a finite resource.

With so many decisions to make every day, we often go with the choice that feels right. It takes a lot of energy to process all the available information before making a choice, so we often rely on a feeling sense about what to do. This means when it comes to choices, more often than not, it's our emotions that are running the show.

If how you feel and how you think are not in alignment with each other, you're in conflict with yourself. Because we get so attached to how we think and feel, we set ourselves up for a lose-lose situation. For example, if you feel like you want to overeat, but think that you shouldn't, one side has to give way to the other – you're either going to overeat or you're not going to overeat. If you overeat, you may have to deal with the mental backlash of 'giving in' and if you don't overeat you'll be sitting with the uncomfortable feeling of wanting to overeat. Quite often the outcome is to just overeat because if you don't it feels like the debate will rage on indefinitely. The feeling part keeps making its demands and if you fight against that feeling, especially if you really don't want to be experiencing it, the desire to escape your emotional discomfort may become overwhelming. When you start wrestling with yourself, eventually mental fatigue sets in and eating seems to be the only way to silence the conflict.

Allowed and disallowed emotions

Emotions were your very first language. Before you were able to use words to think and communicate your thoughts to others, life was a bundle of emotions and you used those emotions to interact with your caregivers. If you were fearful or sad, you cried. If you were happy or delighted, you laughed or smiled. As a baby you didn't know where you ended and the environment began. This is why how we are treated in those early months of life are so developmentally important. Your carers responded to you from their own emotional state, so how you were treated was always more to do with them than you, but as a child you didn't know this. Those early years laid the foundation upon which you started to build a sense of your value and place in the world. These early experiences are stored as preverbal memories, a feeling sense of self, remembered by the body, but without the language needed to consciously access them.

Anyone who has spent time with a three-year-old child will be all too aware that kids at that age are a bundle of uncontained emotions. They can have a complete meltdown about the colour of the straw in their drink, or be inconsolable that someone else is playing with a toy that they didn't want to play with anyway. It's the job of the adults around to teach the child how to tolerate and express their emotions. How this process was managed with you will have shaped the way you experience your emotions today.

Every family has implicit and explicit rules about handling and showing feelings. There will be feelings that are more allowable than others. Depressed and stressed parents can be easily overwhelmed by the emotional demands of a child. Their impatience and frustration with the child's irrationality convey the message that certain feelings, or even feelings in general, are not okay. If our parents struggled with their emotions and couldn't cope with ours, the message often taken in is that, in some way, we are wrong for having these feelings in the first place. What we needed was reassurance and help to manage them, not being punished or pushed away for having them.

This means we learn to suppress the feelings that were seen as bad in our home. For some this could be a suppression of all strong emotions, while for others it could just be certain emotions that were not allowed. We can be so adept at quashing emotions that it may genuinely feel like we don't have them. Vicky was a woman in her forties who told me that she couldn't remember the last time she was angry. 'I'm just not an angry person,' she told me. On exploring further, I discovered that her father had been angry and violent when she was growing up. She told me, 'He would be lovely one moment, but something small could throw him into a rage. If I ever dared to get cross with him, he would go mad. He could always out-anger me. I usually dissolved into helpless tears because he would often calm down quicker if I was crying.' When we looked at what feelings were most familiar to her as an adult, she recognised that if people treated her badly, she felt sad. She struggled to connect to any sense of outrage about being treated unfairly. She had to push her rage down from such a young age that it never gets anywhere near the surface these days.

Where do suppressed feelings go? That is open for debate. There are so many ways of thinking about this and we have no way of measuring suppressed emotions, or their potential impact on us. They might manifest as chronic depression and anxiety due to body and brain chemistry becoming out of sync. Perhaps they express as illnesses; we know there is a link between stress and the deterioration of physical health. They may even morph into different feelings – unfelt sadness may come out as angry and aggressive behaviour.

Advantages of crying

Try to remember the last time you cried. It might have been recently, or it may have been many years ago. What does crying mean to you? There are cultural expectations about crying. Generally, it is still more acceptable for a woman to cry than a man and there are certain situations where it is definitely discouraged, such as in the workplace or on a first date.

I am intrigued by the different attitudes among my clients about crying. Some see therapy as an opportunity to have a really good cry; others are incredibly apologetic at any hint of a sniffle and there are those who talk about the most painful of subjects while remaining utterly stoic. I'm not going to say that anyone *should* cry, but I will say that crying is good for you. Some of the benefits include:

- It works as a pain reliever by releasing an endorphin called leucine-enkephalin.

- Emotional tears contain adrenocorticotropic stress hormones, so you are literally releasing some of the stress chemicals out of you.
- It signals to others that we are in distress, so we are more likely to get support.
- It activates the parasympathetic nervous system, which, as you've heard, calms anxiety and stress.
- Crying helps to keep your eyes clean by producing lysozyme, which kills bacteria.

If food has become the go-to for calming down big emotions, you may want to think about scheduling a good cry. Crying is often associated with losing control, but it's possible to choose to cry. When we embrace a good sob it can be a rewarding experience. During my binge eating days I rarely cried. I felt cut off from the ability to do it, especially if I was alone. Nowadays, I love a good cry. It's like hitting the reset button and when I surrender right into it, I'm rewarded with a sense of calmness and perspective afterwards.

Connecting to how you feel

If you are fed up of using food as your emotional management tool, perhaps it's time to develop a new way of relating to your emotions. Emotions are difficult to write and talk about because they are sensations that we feel. We use sound (speech) and we use shapes (written words) to try to communicate feelings to one another. If you tell me you are feeling anxious, I have to construct a meaning for that word and this involves me drawing on my own experience of feeling anxious, as well as what I have seen in other people or heard about. My interpretation of your anxiety may alter a bit based on how *I'm* feeling in this moment, as well as what I already know about you and whether you are friend, foe...or client.

Language limits us when it comes to exploring, understanding and managing the emotional realm. If you have never been encouraged, or felt able, to talk about how you feel, be patient with yourself. If you don't know how you feel, start by figuring out if this is because you can't connect to the sensations in your body, or if you don't have a word that fits the sensation. (If you do an internet search for the emotional wheel, you will find dozens of printable PDFs, which contain lots of adjectives for different feelings.)

To begin with, you could start with simply noticing if you are feeling pleasant, unpleasant or neutral. This takes the pressure off a bit. As you become more adept at identifying your emotional state you will be able to expand your vocabulary and sense the nuances of your experience.

Have you ever felt low and then met with a cheerful friend who quickly lifted your mood? What about the other way around, when someone else's negativity brings you down? Other people have an influence over how we feel and this can be used to our advantage. Managing our emotions well means having the capacity to self-soothe as well as being able to reach out to other people when we feel like we're struggling. It means being able to tolerate feelings without acting on them and being able to express and release them in an appropriate way.

This is why emotions are so messy. Each emotion takes place in a different context and you are usually trying to figure out what to do about it while you are still in a heightened state of emotion. The ideal place to be is to feel like you have options –

you can choose whether to manage it yourself or connect with someone for support. If you are feeling angry towards someone you have a choice to confront them or tolerate your anger until you feel clearer about the situation.

The idea that you should know what to do with your feelings suggests there is a right and wrong answer. As a therapist, I am reluctant to give advice to anyone about how they should be managing their emotions. My role is to help people understand their emotional experience and feel able to make choices.

Emotions vs. feelings

Although I have used the words 'emotions' and 'feelings' interchangeably throughout the book so far, I want to make a subtle distinction between the two. This can help you navigate your way through your emotional experience and recognise when you can have some influence over your feelings and when they may be beyond your control.

> *Emotions play out in the theatre of the body.*
> *Feelings play out in the theatre of the mind.*
> Dr Sarah McKay

Emotions are a biochemical reaction to an event, created by the lower brain regions, namely the amygdala and ventromedial prefrontal cortices. Some basic emotions are wired into our DNA; hence why there are universal reactions to certain emotions, such as smiling when you are happy, or widening your eyes when surprised. These are not learned reactions to emotions; we see the same responses in people born blind.

If you were being threatened with physical attack, you would probably experience the emotion of fear. You would notice a quickened heart rate, shallow breathing and the release of adrenaline. Emotions are less within our control than our feelings, but because they are a response to an event, if you shift your perception of the event, it is possible to change your emotional reaction to it. This is more difficult to do with events that take you by surprise, but certainly possible with events you can anticipate.

Feelings are processed in a different part of the brain, in the neocortical regions. A feeling is simply an emotion that you assign meaning to. This requires you to perceive an event, have an emotional reaction and then make an interpretation about it. For example, somebody steals your phone (event) and your body creates the biochemistry of anger (emotion). It is possible for all kinds of feelings to follow your initial emotional reaction. You may feel it's unfair (*How dare they?*), you might feel worried (*What if they access my information?*) and you may even feel annoyed with yourself (*I'm so stupid for not paying more attention*).

Just to reiterate, emotions are the physiological response to an event and our feelings are made up of these emotions, plus the context created by our interpretation of the event. Our bodies are always responding to what's happening and we layer meaning upon meaning onto the daily events that make up our lives. When we start to unpick these meanings and question them, that's when we open up the opportunity to create a new outcome.

Let's look at a feeling that's very common in overeaters, the feeling of inevitability. Clients often describe that moment where they know they are going to overeat in the near future. This 'knowing' shifts the tipping point to where it no longer feels possible to go in a different direction; it has now become 'inevitable' that they will overeat. The accompanying thoughts to this feeling go something like this: *I'm going to be home by myself tonight, so I know I'm going to binge,* or *I had some cake this morning and that's ruined the day, so now I know I'll end up buying ice cream on the way home,* or *from the moment I woke up this morning, I just knew it was going to be a bad food day.*

When you are experiencing these moments, what's going to happen next feels inevitable, but it's just a feeling you have constructed from bodily sensations and context. Context in this case is heavily influenced by past experiences, and bodily sensations will include the emotion of anticipation.

In this scenario, you are anticipating an eating event based on your previous experience, which tells you that when you feel like this, you always end up in the food. This could mean that you are adding fear (anxiety) into your biochemical cocktail and maybe a spoonful of disgust too, depending on how negative your self-talk is. When this particular biochemical state has become associated with overeating, it's no wonder it feels inevitable. You have been down this road so many times that you haven't considered you may have missed a turn off. You think you have to continue to the end because that's what you've always done.

What is it that makes us want to escape certain feelings and emotions? Even so-called 'bad' ones may not feel as bad as you think. When we are experiencing any emotion without heaping on a whole load of beliefs about how terrible it is, it's just a sensation in the body that can be open to interpretation. A strong emotional response alerts us that something is happening and, if we can reassure ourselves that whatever is happening does not require us to do anything urgent, it doesn't tend to hang around as long as we expect, but even if it does, it's not necessarily so awful, just a bit uncomfortable.

Meaning moulds our truth

How does it feel to be told, 'don't believe everything you think and don't believe everything you feel'? Depending on your relationship with control, it's either a liberating or scary prospect. It doesn't mean you shouldn't hold beliefs or opinions, or that your feelings aren't real, but it does mean they are subjective, which is great news because this means they are changeable.

We have a need to attribute meaning to our experience and this saves us from annihilism. If nothing means anything, why even be here? Severely depressed people lose all sense of meaning and that's a horrible place to be. People take their own lives due to pain and loss of meaning. We can withstand a lot when we have meaning. Women choose to bear children knowing they will endure the pains of labour, but imagine walking down the street and suddenly being hit with labour pains. If you weren't pregnant you would probably make it mean you were dying. You'd experience a whole new level of terror.

In her book *How Emotions Are Made: The Secret Life of the Brain* Lisa Feldman Barrett writes, 'When you experience [a feeling] without knowing the cause, you are more likely to treat [the feeling] as information about the world, rather than your experience of the world.' The way you feel about the world and the people in it says far more about your own process than it does about anyone or anything else. The way you feel is such a rich source of information about you; paying attention to it can lead you that much closer to understanding yourself and becoming free.

PART TWO

⌘

The RALIC Method™

⌘

Chapter 8

Introducing the RALIC Method

'Never bring the problem solving stage
into the decision making stage.
Otherwise, you surrender yourself to the
problem rather than the solution.'
– Robert H. Schuller

I devised the RALIC method by bringing together the things that helped *me* to break free from compulsive eating. I was already practising something similar to the stages that now make up the method, but I was using them as general intentions and in no particular order. One day, while meditating, the stages came together in my mind – forming the RALIC method. It wasn't exactly an 'a-ha' moment; I hadn't realised anything new, but in that moment the stages merged together into an order which made sense to me. I had created a structure that I could reach for when I was feeling confused or out of control.

The four stages of RALIC came out of a growing realisation that the harder I tried to control food, the more out of control I became. This happened every time. Each time that I let go of trying to control how much I was eating, the bingeing reduced.

When this happened I saw the number on the scale drop by a pound or two, and this would trigger the desire to lose more weight. So I would try to control again and of course, my eating would rebound and before I knew it, I was back in the cycle of bingeing again. This method helped me to break free from my own compulsive eating so I tentatively began to share it with my clients and they started using it to improve their relationship with food as well. I have seen it work in my own life and in the lives of others and this compelled me to write this book to put it out there so it could be found by those who needed it.

Up to this point, this book has been about helping you to increase your understanding of your relationship with food and your body. So far we have looked at developing self-awareness, intuitive eating, why your identity matters and the role of emotions in overeating. An understanding of these areas will support you as you learn how to apply the method.

Psychotherapy can be a frustrating experience for the overeater. Everything makes sense and seems obvious when you are in a cosy therapy room, talking about what happens 'out there.' It's easy to make plans during the session about what you are going to do this week, but you are not in the same state when you are with your therapist as you are when you are facing an evening alone or striding to the shop to get your fix. I have met people who have found therapy to be a shaming experience. They go in week after week, feeling like they've failed again. The therapist becomes an accountability figure and some clients feel compelled to lie to their therapist because they feel so ashamed about not doing what they said they were going to.

Sometimes you get those great 'a-ha' moments in therapy (during my training my course leader called them 'WFMs' – 'wonderful f*cking moments'!). When you see something differently to how you did before, something shifts. A shift in perspective causes a shift in your emotional state too. As soon as you start step one of the RALIC method you create a shift in perspective – you become the observer. Nobody is doing it for you and that is true empowerment. In that moment, you change your identity from the person who is in the experience, to the watcher who is having an experience. It may sound like a very small difference, but we only need to make a small step sideways to see things a little differently.

Think about someone in your life who repeatedly struggles with the same issue. Isn't it easy to see where they keep getting in their own way? Doesn't it seem obvious to you what it is they need to be doing to help themselves? By becoming your own observer, you may be able to see yourself with the kind of perspective you have when it comes to other people's problems.

The greater your self-awareness, and the clearer your intent about what you're trying to do (hopefully that is to become an intuitive eater), the easier it will be to implement the technique. The whole point of RALIC-ing something (yes, I did just turn it into a verb) is to clarify your thoughts and shift your emotional state, because only then can you make a choice about your behaviour. The method is not about trying to trick yourself into wanting to eat less, but about aligning your thoughts and feelings so you can be free to make a choice. You can't change your behaviour from the same thinking and feeling state that you have associated with the old behaviour.

Over the next few chapters we are going to take a deeper dive into each component and look at how to implement them and how they can help you to break free from compulsive eating.

The four steps are:

1. **Recognise**
2. **Accept**
3. **Lean In**
4. **Choose**

Notice your state of being right now. Are you feeling hopeful, cynical or open? Maybe you are reading this on holiday while lying on a sun lounger. Perhaps you are listening to this on a packed train with your face smooshed into someone's armpit. You might be curled up on the sofa with your partner, or in the bedroom hiding from visiting family. Are you currently hungry, full or somewhere in between? Wherever you are, whoever you're with and whatever you're thinking and feeling, all of these factors come together to create your current state of being.

The RALIC method is a way of noticing and shifting this current state, and feeling able to make a clear choice in the moment; a choice that's right for you. As you become familiar with the method you can implement it in other areas of your life, not just those related to eating and body image. Food chaos may be a symptom of what's happening elsewhere in your life. So by using the RALIC steps to manage other challenges and stresses, you'll be able to become very familiar with it and even turn it into a habit.

The RALIC method is NOT a way of manipulating yourself into making a decision not to eat. Its job is to enable you to make a choice from a different state to the one you are usually in just before you overeat. You may still choose to 'overeat', but you shift your state first to make it a choice rather than a compulsion. If you believe you should always use the RALIC method in order to stop yourself from overeating, you'll trigger a conflict between the part of you that wants to overeat and the part of you that doesn't. Each time you do this the battle starts again.

⌘

Chapter 9

The RALIC Method
R is for Recognise

'You'll never be truly happy if you are not
truthful about your unhappiness.'
– Robert Holden

If you master this first step, you master the ability to interrupt self-sabotage. Developing self-awareness is absolutely essential for catching yourself in the moment and recognising what's going on for you. It's about what's going on now, not what went on yesterday. This is the important part to remember. However, you can use the method to work through how you are *feeling* now about what happened in the past.

This step brings awareness to the tension that exists between what's actually happening and what you believe should be happening. If your current reality appears to be in conflict with how you see yourself, or want to see yourself, you need to resolve the dissonance. In order to do this, some part of reality has to be rejected. For example, if you feel lonely, but you believe feeling lonely is shameful, it may be easier to avoid recognising what's going on and instead choose to use food, or other distractions, to escape the reality of feeling lonely.

We will always have blind spots. When I first started training to be a psychotherapist, I was on a mission to remove all my blind spots. My goal was to become a super-aware, self-actualised human being. It took a while (probably longer than it needed to) to realise that having blind spots is an inevitable part of being human. That's not to say we stop looking for them, but rather, accepting that we are not able to know what we don't know. It helps to check in with our willingness to see the parts of us that we are not yet aware of. Doing this opens us up to new possibilities we may not have considered before, and leads us to being more compassionate and tolerant towards ourselves, as well as others.

The pre-binge state

When you see someone you know, the recognition seems to happen instantaneously. The context of the meeting will affect your response to that person; is their presence unexpected, or is this a planned meet up? Your emotional reaction to seeing that person will depend on many things, like your relationship to that person and what happened the last time you were together. Your reaction is influenced by a myriad of factors about the past, the present and your predictions for the immediate future.

The same goes with when you are trying to recognise the moments that you are most vulnerable to overeating. Your current state creates your reality, which in this case is that you are going to overeat. Certain states become strongly associated with certain outcomes. You will have your own unique pre-overeating state where your thoughts, feelings and circumstances all align to make overeating the inevitable result. How you experience this state and the components that create it will vary. Here are some common examples of how thoughts (T), feelings (F) and circumstances (C) combine and lead to an outcome of overeating.

Component 1	Component 2	Component 3	Outcome
I ate a load of biscuits at work today, so I've blown it. (T)	Feels frustrated and like a failure. (F)	Passes a bakery on the way home. (C)	Buys a large quantity of baked goods and binges.
Feels stressed and angry because boss yelled at him today. (F)	Gets home to an empty fridge. (C)	*I need something to feel better.* (T)	Orders pizza, chips and garlic bread. Eats angrily in front of the TV.
Walks pass shop where she usually buys her binge food. (C)	*I'll just pop in and buy dinner. I won't get anything else.* (T)	Feels compulsive urge to buy usual binge foods. (F)	Quickly buys her binge foods as if on autopilot. Goes home and binges.

These are simplified versions of how your pre-overeating state creates the outcome of bingeing. There will be many more factors and influences at play. Some of them will be in your blind spot, so trying to find and dismantle all of them would be tiring work, if even possible.

To take this a little further, let's look at thoughts. Not all thoughts are created equal and we don't always believe them. I remember listening to a radio presenter telling an anecdote about when he met the Queen. He was saying that all he could think about at the time was what would happen if he punched her in the face? He imagined becoming famous worldwide and going down in the history books as the guy who punched the Queen. At no point did he really believe he might do it, but it was an amusing fantasy he played out in his mind. He did not identify with his thoughts so he felt no real compulsion to act on them.

Thoughts alone have very little power until either we believe them or we make some meaning about them. In the recognising stage you identify what you are currently believing and what you are telling yourself about these beliefs.

This method involves getting really honest with yourself. It takes some courage to look at the parts of you that you wish didn't exist. Maybe you are very willing to do this, but without being able to differentiate between when your overeating is problematic and when it is the universal experience of sometimes eating 'too much' you'll continue to feel confused and stuck. To heal from compulsive eating, you need to recognise what is going on and name it. This interrupts your well-worn patterns and draws your consciousness and attention to this very moment. It is only in the moment that there is an opportunity to do something differently, not tomorrow as you keep telling yourself.

These are the five most common events that precede overeating. If you learn to spot these, you'll be able to RALIC them. You need to recognise when you are:

1. Having an urge or sense that you are in danger of overeating.
2. Having a strong emotion that could lead you to food.
3. Not eating enough, or having thoughts about restriction.
4. Treating unhelpful beliefs as facts.
5. About to be, or currently in, a situation you normally associate with overeating.

So it's mid-afternoon and you're noticing that you're having some thoughts about bingeing later. These thoughts are accompanied by that feeling of inevitability and the sense that you 'know' you will be bingeing later. Then you remember you could try to RALIC this. You may be doubtful it will make a difference, but you're willing to try.

I can't begin to stress how helpful it is to say the words out loud, or write them down, during this first step. You may cringe at this but hear me out. When your mind is whirling with anxiety or confusion, through writing or speaking about it you create a bit of space between you and your agitation. When you are in the wanting-to-binge state, all your biases, predictions and old beliefs will be trying to take you over and run the show. My personal preference is to speak what I'm recognising out loud because when I hear my voice, I hear myself amid the chaos in my mind. In public I might have to do it in my head, but if you see me walking down the street and mumbling to myself, I'm probably RALICing something!

When you've decided you're going to RALIC the situation, start with the words, 'I recognise...' and then find your own ending to that sentence. When you've found your first sentence, again say, 'I recognise...', and find a second sentence and then again for a third, a fourth and so on. The number of sentences is not important. What is important is for you to be able to recognise and put into words as much as you possibly can about your current situation and what you are thinking and feeling about it.

In order to get the clearest picture of the moment, begin with recognising the facts of the situation. This is simply where you are and what is happening. This is the objective truth, or at least, something that a hundred people looking at the situation would agree on. So it could be, 'I recognise it's 3 pm...I recognise I am sitting at my desk...I recognise I haven't eaten lunch...' There is no interpretation in these first statements; they are the facts about what's happening.

Next, move onto feelings. Rather than saying, 'I feel...' I would suggest saying, 'I am feeling...' or 'I am having a feeling of...' There is an openness about these phrases that suggests our feelings are changeable, which they are. Instead of 'I feel anxious' it would be 'I am feeling anxious', or even 'I am having a feeling of anxiety' if you prefer. Find a couple of words that feel true to how you are feeling at the time.

Then we look at thoughts. We do thoughts last because it is the area where we can have the most influence. Sometimes it becomes very apparent to you why you are feeling the way you do once you have recognised what you are believing and what you are telling yourself. If you are telling yourself you're out of control, of course you are feeling anxious!

So back to the mid-afternoon scenario where you're having thoughts about overeating later. In this situation, recognition may look something like this:

- I recognise I am sitting at my desk.
- I recognise I am going to go home to an empty house.
- I recognise I am feeling uncomfortable and agitated.
- I recognise I am having a feeling of inevitability.
- I recognise I am believing my feelings and believing I will binge later.
- I recognise I am telling myself it's inevitable I will binge tonight.
- I recognise I am believing nothing will ever change.
- I recognise I am telling myself there's no point in fighting it.
- I recognise...

When finding your statements, write or say 'I recognise' before you even know how the sentence is going to end. We don't often start a sentence without knowing which direction it's going to go in. Doing this is like asking your brain a question. Because you're starting a statement that you don't know the answer to, you create an expectation for your mind to go off and find an answer for you. This opens you up to discovering something new. Ideally you keep saying 'I recognise' until you run out of things to recognise. The last thing you say will be an incomplete sentence, just the words 'I recognise...' trailing off at the end.

In order for this to work, you'll need to frame any judgement statements carefully. A judgement statement is treating a subjective belief as an indisputable fact. For example, a client might be sharing their RALIC process with me and they'll say something like, 'I recognise I am being ridiculous.' This isn't helpful because it doesn't come from the observer. The part of you that is judging it to be ridiculous is speaking here. We need to move into the observer mode in order to shift perspective. It may feel true to you that this is ridiculous, but this needs to be recognised for what it is – a belief that feels like it's true. The recognition statement in this instance would be something like, 'I recognise I am telling myself I am being ridiculous.' Or 'I recognise I am believing I am being ridiculous.' Both statements acknowledge the part of you that thinks your struggle with eating is ridiculous, but leaves a bit of space for a different interpretation.

Doing the method after a binge

If you recognise something is happening, but you quickly judge it to be catastrophic, the reaction will usually be to hastily push it aside. You are judging yourself so quickly that it's hard to recognise the benefit of recognising. You don't want to pause and try to understand, because it's too uncomfortable – you may be making the situation, or your response to it, mean something bad about you as a person. If so, this is your self-critical voice getting in your way. Some people become frustrated in the early stages because they go away feeling motivated to use the RALIC method between sessions, but then a week passes and they realise they didn't do it once. Some self-compassion and patience is absolutely vital when it comes to developing the ability to interrupt your usual patterns.

If you keep missing the pre-binge moment – don't worry, this will probably happen in the beginning. You are learning something new and RALIC can be done any time before, during or after a binge, but it's always about the *now*. It's not a retrospective technique, you always work with it in the present, but even if you've already binged you can work through what's going on for you now. Start recognising. You're trapped in a cycle so the method can be used at any stage. It may make sense for you to work with the aftermath first. It's difficult to implement something new when you are in the throes of an urge to overeat; sometimes afterwards is when you may feel more open to giving it a go.

Post-binge recognition might look something like this:

- I recognise I ate [insert specifically what you have eaten, no judgement words like 'too much', 'loads' or 'a lot'. Keep to the facts.]
- I recognise I am having feelings of disappointment/ frustration/failure.
- I recognise I am feeling uncomfortable/stuffed/fat.
- I recognise I am believing this to be wrong/a problem/ not what I want to be doing.
- I recognise I am telling myself I must make up for it tomorrow.
- I recognise...

Anticipation can help you to plan ahead for the moments you'd like to remember to RALIC. Building awareness of your patterns, your triggers and the situations that usually evoke a desire to overeat will help you with this step. If you know you are usually prone to overeating when faced with an evening on your own, or at a particular time of day, you might plan in advance when to use the RALIC method. Some people use timers on their mobile phones to remind them to take a moment to recognise what's going on; or you could put a Post-It sticker somewhere you'll notice it (it can be blank, as long as you know what it's for). Finding ways to remember will be helpful if life is very busy, or you know you spend a lot of your day not being present.

As soon as you consciously notice and name your experience you've set an intention to recognise your reality. Your intention has shifted from being fully invested in your experience to wanting to understand it. It really is the most important step because without it, the other steps just don't make sense. The other steps can't work without recognising what you are working the steps on. Nowadays when I RALIC, I don't always get to the next steps. There are occasions when I do this first step – I recognise what's happening inside and outside of me – and immediately I feel released and free to make a choice because I'm not identified with my experience anymore, it's just an experience. This tends to happen with familiar situations or events where I have previously worked through the whole method.

Body image

If you are struggling with body image, RALICing can be a useful tool to shift you towards a place of acceptance and peace. I hope by now you understand the importance of accepting your body as it is today, but if this is difficult for you, hang in there, we're going to revisit it in the next chapter. If body acceptance sounds hard or even impossible, I get it; I resisted it for years.

It's okay if you doubt your ability to do it, and it doesn't matter if you don't know how you'll do it. My question to you is this: are you willing to try? The alternative is staying where you are and allowing the conflict with how your body looks to roll on and on.

Let's look at an example of how you might use recognition when it comes to body image. Perhaps a friend takes a photograph of you on a night out. She shows you the photo and when you see it, a strong and unpleasant feeling arises. You see a double chin, you see arms that look too big, and that outfit you thought looked 'flattering' in the mirror seems to cling in all the wrong places. Your mind goes straight to thoughts and judgements about how awful you look. You can't believe you've let yourself get to this place and you start thinking that you need to lose weight.

Stop. Breathe. What's going on?

- I recognise I am looking at a photo somebody took of me.
- I recognise I am feeling fat/anxious/angry/panicky.
- I recognise I am believing it to be a bad photo.
- I recognise I am believing I look horrible.
- I recognise I am telling myself that my body should not look this way.
- I recognise I am telling myself that the solution to this experience is to change the way my body looks.
- I recognise...

That's it for this step. You recognise as much as you can about the situation and your thoughts and feelings around it. You don't need to change anything right now; you are merely catching yourself and noticing what's going on.

Stay with the present

While you want to recognise the full picture of your reality, it can be easy to go too far off-piste when searching for your 'I recognise' statements. More may not always be better. You'll want to find as many as you can in order to capture the moment, but try to confine it to your experience right now. Sometimes when people start recognising, they move into recognising other things that are being triggered in the present, but aren't about now. This can take you further and further from the present, unravelling layers and recognising things that go back to a previous toxic situation, or events from your childhood. You don't want to tumble down the rabbit hole by pulling up things from the last days, months or years. If you find yourself doing this, let your next statement be about recognising what you are doing, e.g. 'I recognise I am dredging up lots of past hurts.' This helps bring you back to now.

If at any point, you think you're doing it wrong simply recognise you are *believing* you're doing it wrong, or say that you're having a belief that you're doing it wrong. Your mind will want to push on and make interpretations about the things you're recognising. Watch out for this. Keep bringing your statements back to what you can recognise about this moment.

In this stage you are simply noticing and naming, preferably out loud or in writing. You do not need to figure out what your options are. Without understanding where you currently are, you can't figure out which direction to go in. You may think you know what your options are, but by remaining open, something new may arise. Your rational brain might be good at listing potential choices you could make, but your choices aren't really choices if they don't feel viable in the moment. You know rationally that when you are overeating, in theory, you should be able to stop at any point, even if you've just started, but does this feel possible? If it did you'd have a much easier time stopping unwanted eating and you probably wouldn't be reading this book now. The RALIC method is a way to make your choices feel less like habit or compulsion, and more like real choices.

⌘

Chapter 10

The RALIC Method
A is for Accept

'You can fight with reality, and you'll
only lose 100% of the time.'
– Byron Katie

Imagine for one moment that you are in the city of Edinburgh. However, you don't want to be there, you want to be in London. So you sit around all day, noticing everything that's wrong with Edinburgh and wishing you were in London. Because you don't want to be there, you never take the time to explore the city, build relationships with other residents, or allow yourself to see any of the positives. You're afraid if you did you'd end up stuck there, never making it to where you really want to be. You swing from one day hoping that you will be able to move to London to the next, despairing that nothing will ever change.

Refusing to accept your body today is like living somewhere you hate and wishing you were somewhere else. You can't see the wonderful parts about where you are because you are too busy thinking about how you would prefer things to be. You convince yourself your real life can only start once you are living in a slim body.

If one day you decide to drive to London, without first accepting you are in Edinburgh, you will have no idea which direction you need to head in. You may not like where you are starting from, but without acknowledging the reality of where you are, how can you even begin the journey?

Your journey to freedom from overeating is the same. You may be feeling very impatient about getting to the promised land. Of course, if you were actually driving the 400 miles from Edinburgh to London, you could plot out your route in advance, but there is no exact route for your journey when it comes to food and body image. You simply need to set off and trust you'll figure it out along the way.

Understanding acceptance

Before we dive into how the RALIC method approaches the issue of acceptance, I want to highlight some of the things it is not:

- It's not passivity.
- It's not being a victim of circumstance.
- It's not the same as approving of something.
- It's not resigning yourself to the situation.
- It's not giving up personal responsibility.

There are always two components to your reality – the circumstances and your reaction to the circumstances. Your reactions occur on so many levels; your initial reaction may not be within your conscious control because it's largely conditioned by the past. But then, once you become aware, you have the opportunity to react to this reaction. This is the beauty of being an evolving human being and also, this is why step one has to be recognition.

When you recognise, you see how you continue to pick fights with how things are, and you do this because they are in opposition to how you think things should be. I see this all the time when it comes to how people respond to their hunger. If they don't believe they should be hungry (*I only ate two hours ago!*), or they don't want to be hungry (*I need to lose weight, I mustn't give in*), then they tell themselves that they shouldn't be hungry. They may seek distraction or try to convince themselves that they do not need to eat. Either way, their appetites start fighting back. Food obsession and out-of-control eating is usually the result.

Acceptance is simply deciding not to argue with reality anymore. It means no longer fighting with, or running away from, the truth of right now. You are accepting what's happening only because it *is* happening. You are not giving up; you are simply acknowledging what is going on right now – not accepting an imagined future. This is the most important part to understand about this step. Your mind will try to tell you that accepting a situation means nothing will ever change, but in truth, when you accept something, *you* change. This is great news because change always starts with you.

Letting go

Why do so many of us find acceptance such a challenge? Well, for starters, it means letting go. Trying to exert self-control when you are feeling out of control seems to make a lot of sense. Letting go appears counterintuitive because you think it means you will feel out of control instead.

Every single thing you have eaten up until this very moment is no longer within your control. Take a moment to consider this. All that energy you have spent beating yourself up about your past food choices has been energy spent on arguing with something that is beyond your control. You have an appetite for food. You cannot change the fact you have an appetite and that your appetite fluctuates. You have tried to dominate it and this only made it more powerful. There is a part of your brain that knows how to undermine your will at any hint of restriction, so you keep losing control each time you try to push back or ignore your hunger.

You can argue with yourself about whether you should or shouldn't have eaten something, but that's in the past. By refusing to accept this, all you'll do is prolong your misery and make yourself anxious or depressed about your eating. This is going to make it harder to make wise decisions about your food in the present. You may believe beating yourself up is the only way to force yourself to make better food decisions, but how's that been working out for you so far?

Think of all the times you have planned to eat less tomorrow in order to 'make up' for what you've eaten today. Those were restrictive thoughts and these can trigger forces that are capable of taking you over, so you end up bingeing in reaction to anticipated restriction. It's challenging because you believe you should be able to simply decide how much you put in your mouth. Other people seem to be able to do this, so why can't you? Maybe you just can't. Because you end up bingeing when you do. Because your brain and biology has found a way to override your will to restrict your food intake. Your instinct to eat had to ramp up higher because you have been trying to cage it. It took the reins away from you in an attempt to protect you from self-imposed starvation.

Denial and comparison

When we don't accept something we have to reject and deny it. Denial is a common way of managing loss and grief. During my bereavement work I often came across people who had lost loved ones and were struggling to accept that the deceased had gone for good. There was some acceptance, otherwise they wouldn't have been coming for grief counselling in the first place. They knew in their rational brain that the person had died, but another part, a feeling part, had not caught up with this yet.

Accepting something we wish wasn't true means letting go of the idea of a different reality – a reality where a deceased loved one is still alive, or perhaps a reality where you effortlessly lose weight and everyone starts treating you differently. Even though this alternate reality doesn't exist, you may have been invested in the idea of it for a long time. The belief in this version of reality may have kept you going during difficult times. Saying goodbye to it may feel like saying goodbye to an old friend.

The image in your mind about what your life would look like without food or weight worries is just that, an image. If you believe people will care about you more, or if you think you'll be fearless, socially confident and happier, you may be setting yourself up for a big disappointment. If you want to move forwards, you may need to accept this. You might need to take some time to grieve for the loss of the illusion.

You may look at other people's reality and want what they have. The thing is, we can never really know what someone else's reality is. We can look at their circumstances – their job, appearance, relationships etc. – and think we know what their reality must be like. It looks pretty good to us, but as we now know, reality is not just external. It's our response to reality that creates our experience of it. Comparing yourself to others leaves you feeling either superior or inferior. It feels pretty rubbish when you judge yourself to be inferior, but feeling superior is a fragile state because it relies on other people struggling in order to feel okay about yourself.

Seeing someone else doing what you believe you keep failing at, and using this as a means to berate yourself, is to keep comparing yourself and coming up short. You cannot draw meaningful conclusions about yourself by comparing your perceived shortfalls to your perception of others' abilities. We never know what's really going on with someone. We're all so different; there are too many variations and we have no objective tool to measure the worth and value of a person.

Our egos are very good at convincing us that we know more than we actually do. We tell ourselves we know what we're supposed to be doing and what will bring us happiness. Well, nothing can bring happiness to you. Happiness is a state, not something given to us by circumstances; nor is it a place we finally arrive at when we've fixed all our problems. Researchers in Stockholm found the day-to-day happiness levels of lottery winners did not increase after they won a truckload of money. There would be a peak in happiness levels after their win, but within a year, they reported being no happier than they were before they won the money.

It's often the same when it comes to weight loss. It can be a real buzz to get down to a particular number on the scale and bask in the compliments from people, but the compliments soon dry up, and the excitement dims. Your food demons didn't go anywhere. Food is still the enemy and now you're even more fearful of it because the thought of gaining the weight back is terrifying.

How we feel has far more to do with the conversations we have in our heads than anything going on outside of us. The way you think about your life is what dictates the quality of your existence. You may want something outside of you to change before you can feel better. As we saw with the lottery winners, that doesn't usually work in the long term, so why wait for something that's available to you right now?

Stopping the struggle

Because we think we know more than we do, it's very easy for our minds to lead us in the wrong direction. Believing something doesn't make it true. If you believe your thoughts and your thoughts tend to be pretty self-critical, you'll be especially vulnerable to creating unreasonable expectations of yourself. You won't even realise they are unreasonable though, because you think you know it's true. This means you'll wander through life, never feeling like you're good enough, no matter how hard you're trying.

When it came to my own binge eating, I thought recovery was about getting rid of all urges to binge. For years I was adamant this must be possible because I would occasionally experience a couple of binge-free weeks, where I wasn't even thinking about food. During these times, I would get excited that I had finally conquered my problem, but then, seemingly out of the blue, usually around the two or three week mark, I would fall back into the cycle of overeating again. It always seemed so sudden; I could never understand how it happened and it would blindside me every time. I'd feel devastated; it wasn't fair! Why did this keep happening to me? Couldn't the universe, fate or God see how hard I was trying and just give me a break!? It would then be followed by several weeks, or even months, of bingeing and feeling even more out of control than ever.

Today I have accepted that a shadowy version of binge thoughts may visit from time to time, but I no longer struggle with them. This is more freeing than if I had managed to chase them away, or than if they had just vanished on their own. If I needed the urges to go away in order to be okay with food, then I would always be at their mercy should they decide to return.

I no longer identify as someone who struggles with their eating anymore. I'm good at recognising unhealthy urges and I always have the RALIC method to turn to if I ever feel like I am getting lost again. Once I recognise and accept an urge to eat compulsively, it tends to vanish. Other times I may work through all the steps.

To believe that I should be in a place where I never feel the urge to overeat again is to keep fighting with the reality of my experience. Certain circumstances tend to throw up old thoughts, but when these thoughts appear they seem separate to me now and further away than they used to be. I don't have the same emotional response to them anymore, so they don't feel dangerous. Maybe one day they will go away completely.

Maybe they won't. I can honestly say I don't mind either way. In fact, part of me thinks it's better if the urges never totally vanish. My struggle with compulsive eating is such an important part of who I am today and it has become my purpose to help others who are still struggling.

So I don't want to forget what it was like.

I don't want to lose my humility.

Your acceptance speech

It's okay if the acceptance stage only feels like a cognitive exercise. As long as your thinking brain sees the necessity of acceptance and is willing to accept that the feelings just haven't caught up yet, then that's good enough. Acceptance is a process and it's easy to become frustrated if you want to accept, but you're still struggling to actually do it. For many people, acceptance is a gradual thing that requires them to tolerate their doubt and frustration and keep coming back to the intention to accept. The more often you practise acceptance, the better you get at it; it's a skill that can be honed.

Once you've identified your recognition statements, it's time to figure out how you can accept them. Remember, you are only accepting what is happening right now. You don't need to change a thing and you don't need to work out what to do next. You have probably been trying to find out how to fix your overeating for a long time and if you're reading this book, that probably hasn't worked so far. This is a chance to try something new.

You need to figure out what will help you to accept. You know which arguments for acceptance resonate with you the most, so what would you need to remember in the moment? You can write your own acceptance speech by gathering key phrases and ideas that speak to you and feel true. I encourage people to have a few sentences that start with 'Of course...' It immediately changes the energy around any phrase. Here are some snippets from other people's acceptance speeches:

- 'Of course I am going to feel like this because I have felt like this so often before.'
- 'Of course I'm feeling anxious/tired/frustrated because this is just how I'm feeling.'
- 'Of course I don't know that this isn't how things are supposed to be right now.'
- 'Of course I need to feel this in order to move through it.'
- 'Of course I can accept this now because it won't last forever.'
- 'Of course I accept this because it's my reality and I choose reality over avoidance. That's something I can control.'
- 'Of course this is supposed to happen because it *is* happening.'
- 'Of course I am feeling conflicted about this.'
- 'Of course I want to feel happy more than I want to be right.'
- 'Of course I've forgotten again that I can't control this.'

You might think you are doing acceptance wrong if you aren't instantly transported to a state of peace. This is not true. This stage is about the willingness to change your viewpoint, even if you don't know how to yet. Sometimes you will feel peace, but if you are only accepting in order to create a particular emotion, this is conditional acceptance. If the desired emotion doesn't come, you'll either feel cheated or you'll blame yourself for not doing it right. Doing this step well means accepting the reality and letting emotional outcome be what it is.

It's been said that the secret to happiness is lowering your expectations. Although this tends to be said with some cynicism, it has a ring of truth to it. It's not caring less or giving up, but recognising we often have expectations that are unrealistic. Our culture insists that hard work will be rewarded. You are taught to believe that if you're not seeing the results you want, then you should be putting more work in. So if you're not sticking to the diet, you should be trying harder.

Stop expecting reality to be other than it is. When you stop making demands that you and the world should be different and when you accept, really accept, the reality of the current moment, you stop wasting energy fighting against that which is beyond your control. This frees you up to be able to take action on the things you can influence and make peace with the things you can't.

'There comes a time when you look into the mirror and you realize that what you see is all that you will ever be. And then you accept it [...].Or you stop looking in mirrors.'
- Tennessee Williams

⌘

Chapter 11

The RALIC Method
LI is for Lean In

'Face your life, its pain, its pleasure, leave no path untaken.'
– Neil Gaiman

Initially this stage might be the trickiest concept to grasp. There are a few different ways of thinking about what this step entails, so this chapter is about helping you to find your own understanding of what 'leaning in' means for you. Broadly speaking, leaning in means embracing an experience, which then leads you to a deeper understanding; rather than something you need to understand first, *before* you can have the experience. This process is beyond words, but words are the only tools I have to be able to share this concept, so I'll do my best for you.

How to feel

This step is about feeling your feelings. You do this by moving towards the present moment; the moment you have already recognised and accepted. It involves pushing your awareness into any feelings or sensations in your body and letting your thoughts land where they will. There is no need to try to work out what you're feeling. If words arise, that's fine. They may be helpful, but if you notice you're having a conversation in your head about what's going on, then your attention may have moved away from the feelings and into your thinking mind instead. Just notice what you're doing and bring your awareness right back into the centre of what's happening in your body.

One of the common personality traits in people who overeat is something that psychologists have called a *low tolerance for discomfort*. I don't think this is a helpful term, because it seems to suggest that people who overeat can't cope with their emotions like everyone else can, so they run to the food at any sign of discomfort. I believe there is more to it. If overeating has been a long and weary struggle, it may be that the mind responds to the emotions in a way that is like pouring petrol over a naked flame. Certain emotions become catastrophic because they have been made to mean something terrible about either the person themselves or the situation. Their emotions and beliefs collide, exploding into an unbearable experience. This may be what feels intolerable, not simply the emotions themselves.

Eating can become a coping mechanism for difficult feelings but so can any other addiction, as well as the numerous distractions like TV, phones and even active pursuits and hobbies. I would suggest that the majority of us have a low tolerance for discomfort. We may be willing to choose it if the perceived pay-off seems worth it, but not many of us choose to feel uncomfortable if we can avoid it. Moving towards how you feel is a bit like choosing the feeling, or at least choosing to feel the feeling. You may be wondering why you would feel uncomfortable for no apparent pay-off? What you are really choosing is reality. Whatever the feelings are, they are there and they want to be felt. You can keep running and distracting, but to do this you have to keep abandoning yourself.

Your mind might start to get busy when you lean in to your experience. It wants to figure out what this is and why you're doing it. Of course it does! That's your mind's job. But if you keep getting lost in your thoughts, just notice again and bring your attention back to the body. If this doesn't seem to be working, you can go back to step one and recognise this keeps happening and then start working through the stages on whatever is emerging for you. This would mean interrupting the leaning in with new recognition statements, 'I recognise I am getting caught up in my thoughts. I recognise I am finding this step difficult, I recognise…etc.' Then move through the second step by accepting that you keep moving into your thoughts and that you are finding the third step challenging. Then lean in to the experience of this. You may feel frustrated with this step. Great! Move towards the centre of that frustration and greet it like the old friend that it is.

This stage is more than just sitting back and allowing your feelings, it's moving towards them with open arms and a willingness to accept them. You may have been struggling with not feeling acceptance during the second step. No problem at all. Move into the feeling of struggle, resistance or whatever the sensation is. Keep moving closer to it. If you feel an urge to move away, move into that urge. Notice how it feels and how it moves and shifts.

The urge to escape

It's no great revelation to say that we live in a world of distractions. From mobile phones to on-demand TV, mood-altering substances to compulsive behaviours, never before have we had so much choice about how to distract ourselves, nor have the methods to do so ever been more readily available to us.

One of the biggest psychological pay-offs to overeating is that it creates the ability to escape. When eating turns compulsive you are no longer attached to the present. You may feel numb or unconscious, or frantic and stimulated. Whatever you feel while overeating, it will be different to how you would feel if you were being fully present with yourself. If you want to break free from compulsive eating, finding a way to be with yourself, without having to turn to distractions, is the path to freedom.

What compels so many of us to seek out ways of escaping ourselves? As the French philosopher Blaise Pascal wrote, 'All of humanity's problems stem from man's inability to sit quietly in a room alone.' This was written back in the 1600s, so the drive to distract is far from just a product of the modern world. But if we can learn to sit with ourselves without whipping out our phones, or falling into destructive overconsumption, we really can solve the majority of our problems, certainly the mind-made ones, which let's face it, are most of them.

If you think about the common ways people distract themselves, you might think of shopping, eating, watching TV, playing video games or scrolling through social media. We don't need to label these as bad in and of themselves, but it is helpful to understand how you use them and to what end. When your life revolves around moving from one distraction to the next you end up spending the majority of your time in a semi-conscious state, being brought into the present only when pain, discomfort or excitement grabs your attention.

You'll find you only feel present when you are feeling high or when you are feeling low. When you live mainly in the highs or lows of life it's a pretty safe bet to assume you are someone who has a tendency towards black-and-white thinking – you're either being really 'good' with your eating or you're being 'terrible'. The RALIC method challenges this style of thinking. So be patient with yourself and take a moment to look at how you are feeling about the method so far. If you approach it with an all-or-nothing mindset, you'll think it either sounds brilliant or rubbish. It doesn't have to be either of those things. It's just a tool. On its own it won't change anything – you get to test it out and decide for yourself whether to make a commitment to becoming a skilled RALIC user.

Black-and-white thinking is a way of trying to create certainty. If you can say with confidence that something is one thing or another, you can feel as if you understand things that would otherwise be messy and confusing. Most things in life come in shades of grey, and if your world has always looked black and white, it can be really challenging to see the grey. When I ask my clients to find the grey in a particular scenario, to begin with they are stumped. They genuinely can't find a grey option. It doesn't seem to exist if you don't know what the middle ground looks like. Learning to see the grey is like learning anything new, it gets easier with practice and a bit of help.

Creating a mental spectrum can help. If hating your body is a 1 on the scale and loving your body is 100, what would be a 2, 28 or 70? Most situations can be put on a spectrum. It may feel like your brain isn't cooperating very well when you start doing this. Don't panic. It's only because your brain isn't used to looking for the middle ground. Enlist other people to help you with this; ask them what they think and notice the difference in how we all interpret situations. Don't choose a fellow all-or-nothing thinker though! Pick someone who you see as balanced and flexible in their approach to life.

Being present with what is, especially when 'what is' doesn't appear to be very exciting, can feel like sitting in the grey. I used to be very all-or-nothing in my approach to life. I was either super busy, or crashed out watching TV and eating. Both were a means of trying to escape the middle ground, which to me felt utterly mundane and boring. Some of the words my clients have used to describe the middle ground include agitated, restless, doom and nothingness.

If this resonates with you, you'll notice that being present has become associated with feeling uncomfortable. Part of you has come to fear this state of discomfort, so the last thing you would usually do is choose to sit with that moment and just let it be.

Needing more (and more)

Some people find this stage the hardest part to get the hang of. Jess was a 32-year-old woman with a busy job and an even busier social life. She would fill every moment of her day and she recognised that she found it impossible to stop doing things because when she did, she would experience waves of loneliness. When she leaned into the loneliness, she understood something deeper about herself. 'I realised that if I just sit in the mundane, I'm faced with my mortality,' she told me. 'Every day I wake up closer to death. Life is a finite resource and I want to live my life under bright lights. I'm always looking for my place to shine. There's this never-ending desire to want more.'

There is a well-known satirical quip that goes something like, 'What is it that people always want, no matter what they have?' The answer? More. We strive and push and acquire and compare, and for what? We never get there; we never have enough; we never are enough. We believe we need to be more attractive, lose more weight. Our family should be more loving and people should be more appreciative about what we do for them.

The Recognise, Accept and Lean In stages are all about facing and accepting the current truth of the present. We do this because fighting against it just doesn't work. You're experiencing your reality, whether you like it or not. Why make the experience more painful than it already is by trying to push against it? If that worked you would have made all the changes you wanted by now and life would be exactly how you wanted it to be, or at least, *you* would be exactly how you wanted to be. I want to stress again that you are only bringing an attitude of acceptance to your current truth; this moment, right now. If you have cognitively accepted your truth, then that sets you up to be willing to feel your truth, which is what leaning in is all about.

I played around with the idea of calling this stage Surrender. I like the idea of surrender, but it doesn't sit well with everyone. In a dominate-or-be-dominated culture, surrender can sound like weakness or giving up. Wars often end with one side surrendering and this side is considered the loser. However, the reason why one side is willing to surrender is because the death count is rising and the cost of continuing the war has become too high. If you decide to continue to fight for control, your mental health is going to become the collateral damage. That's an enormous price to pay. When you surrender to the present moment, you are surrendering both sides of the conflict because you are both sides of the conflict. Let's call a truce and use this as an opportunity to create a peace treaty with ourselves.

Lean in and listen

Your emotions are calling out for your attention. If you have been ignoring them or stuffing them down with food, it may take a bit of time to notice the sensations and figure out what the concept of moving towards them means to you. Putting your attention right in the centre of how you feel means your emotions get to fulfil their job, which is to get your attention. Emotions are biochemical messages in the body; they move and morph, shift and change. Leaning in to them acknowledges their existence, which allows them to be expressed, instead of repressed.

If it feels like nothing is going on, lean in to that sense of nothingness. If it feels like you are stuck, lean in to the stuckness. There is a conflict going on, which keeps splitting your attention. Being stuck sometimes feels like nothing is happening, but stuckness is usually your mind pushing in different directions at the same time. Imagine an ongoing game of tug-of-war with no clear winners. It may look like not much is happening, but a huge amount of energy is being expended by both sides. It's an exhausting way to live. Resolution will only come by putting down the rope and stepping away.

The whole point of the RALIC method is to feel able to let go of the conflict. This may be temporary to begin with. If one side of the conflict wins, a part of you has to lose, so it cannot be resolved peacefully in this way. When you recognised, you awoke the observer; when you accepted, you engaged your mental willingness to view things differently; and now, when you lean in, you connect with the messages in the body. We hold emotional memories that are not attached to words or images; this makes them hard to access at will. We can't force it. We can only pay attention to them and move in to greet whatever arises.

⌘

Chapter 12

The RALIC Method
C is for Choose

'We don't get to choose what is true.
We only get to choose what we do about it.'
– Kami Garcia

Freedom should be a fundamental birth right. As humans, we place a very high value on being free. Up until now it's very likely that you have been trying to manage your overeating by setting yourself rules – *Stop eating this, don't eat that, just eat less dammit!* When you do this, you keep taking away your own freedom. You've lost faith in yourself, so you doubt your ability to handle the freedom to eat what you want.

You may have underestimated how strong the desire to feel free is.

The idea of giving yourself full permission when it comes to food can sound very scary. You think you cannot control yourself so you imagine that if you weren't trying to restrain yourself, then you'd really be in trouble. Even if you are currently overeating on a frequent basis, you're not truly giving yourself permission to eat. You just grab windows of opportunity here and there while, at the same time, feeling like you shouldn't be doing it. You know that feeling of abandonment when you break the rules and go on a binge? You think it's just about wanting the food, but perhaps it's also about wanting to be free.

Free to choose

You're here because you want something to change. Chances are, you want to stop overeating and you want to change your body. You are reading a book called *I Can't Stop Eating*. If the title resonates with you, you know what it's like to feel unable to make a choice to stop eating. You tell yourself *I must stop eating*, but as soon as you believe you must you're no longer free.

You may believe the answer is simply to find a way of eating less food, but rather than trying to force a behavioural change you'll need to stop predetermining what those choices are supposed to be. Lasting change involves changing the process you normally go through that keeps leading you to the same place – compulsive eating.

The steps so far are designed to create a shift in your mindset so that you are making a decision from an altered state to the one you're usually in before you overeat. You think you know what food decisions you should be making, but those beliefs come from a mind that is used to feeling either in control or out of control when it comes to food.

When you've had a period of chaotic eating and you manage to summon enough willpower to get your eating back under control, it can feel soooo good. You believe this should be your natural state, but this is the part that deceives so many people. You've dieted before so you should be able to do it again, right? You were sugar-free/paleo/keto for a few months once, so you believe it should be possible for you to live this way all the time. Because you have experienced times of being in control it therefore seems logical to you that this is the way you need to be. You blame yourself when you don't manage to do it consistently. However, it's like holding your breath; you can do it for a bit with no problems, but eventually your brain and body will rebel, no matter how high your determination is.

The RALIC method will have limited value if you are trying to use it to conquer your appetite, but it can be used to bring you into a place where you are no longer dominated by a seemingly insatiable desire for food. It all comes back to that middle ground again. If you are still struggling with the concept of needing to have control over your appetite, self-sabotage will continue. I know the desire to control may not disappear overnight; it's been a part of you for a long time. Your role is to recognise when this desire comes back again. If it starts to creep in, using the RALIC method on the urge to control itself can give you the perspective you need to be able to make a choice about whether to let it go again.

If you have understood the RALIC method to be a way of stopping yourself from overeating, you may find that you feel resistant to using it in the moments when it would benefit you the most. RALIC is not a way to trick yourself into not eating or making a 'purer' food choice. The intention, which may need to be repeated often in order to hold it at the forefront of your mind, is to free yourself to make a choice. If you are deciding ahead of time what you should be choosing, it's not a choice. As soon as you believe you should be making a particular choice any alternative choice feels less viable, so might as well not be a choice at all.

So what is the choice you're trying to make? It's tempting to believe that the choice has to involve an action, such as choosing what to eat and then following through with that choice. This step is more than that; you have so many options to consider. Choice can be deciding to postpone a decision. For example, if you're feeling very confused about what to eat, you may decide to wait ten minutes and see whether you get a feeling for what you want. Choice may also be choosing your attitude towards something. It may mean choosing to stay and tolerate the discomfort, or doing something to soothe your feelings. You may also choose to do something that you normally associate with escapism, but instead, you mindfully choose it, as opposed to being compelled to do it as an avoidance technique.

Making wise decisions

How do you tend to make decisions? Are you someone who goes with their gut feeling, or do you need to consider all the available information first? If you are the latter, making food choices this way is exhausting because there is an almost limitless amount of information you could draw on, not to mention all the contradictory messages in nutrition research. Listening to your body's wisdom is learning to trust that your body has all the information you need to make a wise choice for you.

Intuitive eating is about tapping into our intuition and using it to make the choice that's right for us, in the moment. Intuition is the ability to understand something instinctively, without conscious reasoning. It's a feeling response, but in order to hear it we need to be able to understand our dilemma (recognise), stop fighting with our current situation (accept) and be willing to experience it (lean in). These first three steps help to create a state where you are better able to connect with your eating instincts. This doesn't mean learning to respond perfectly to your physical requirements; you will still sometimes feel like you have eaten too much or wish you had eaten more, but when you keep centreing yourself through listening, being and letting go you will develop your own understanding of how to nourish yourself with food – physically, mentally, emotionally and socially.

Your body contains an innate wisdom when it comes to what it needs to eat. The body cannot speak to you in words; it speaks in sensations, which the mind needs to interpret in order to take the appropriate action. For example, you could be sitting at home watching television. You get up to get a blanket from another room and return to your position. What probably preceded this action was an awareness of feeling chilly and an image of the blanket in the next room, so you went to get it and life moved on. This is how our eating can be. A physical sensation (hunger), an idea of how to respond to the situation (food option), carrying it out (eating) and life moves on. Back to the blanket example – on a different day you may consciously choose to keep the blanket next to you in case you need it, or even drape it over yourself before you feel cold. Again, it's the same with food. A healthy relationship with food can include having a plan in case you get hungry and will sometimes involve anticipatory eating, which is eating before you feel hungry because you know you are likely to feel hungry soon.

How we decide

There are two types of decision-making processes and both use different parts of your brain. There are habit decisions – these are made in an area deep in the brain called the basal ganglia – and there are value-based decisions, which are made at the front of our brains in our prefrontal cortex.

Habit decisions are all the things you do on autopilot. The classic and well-worn example is brushing your teeth before you go to bed. It might not feel like it, but this is a decision. Because the prefrontal cortex isn't involved there's no conscious thinking going on; your subconscious brain is deciding for you. I suspect that the brain is especially adapted to turn eating and drinking into automated behaviours because they are the most important things we do after breathing, which is of course, an automated behaviour too. You can choose to hold your breath for a bit, but eventually, regardless of how strong willed you are, your brain will force you to breathe. I think it's the same with eating.

The value-based decisions are the ones we make to get a certain outcome, or to achieve a goal or aim. We need to weigh up information to make this kind of decision and this means using the orbitofrontal cortex, which is located right behind your forehead. I have a friend who used to be a competitive kickboxer. She received a hard kick to her forehead once and lost the ability to make decisions for a few days. She told me that someone could offer her the choice between a yoghurt or a piece of fruit and she would dissolve into tears because she just couldn't make a decision, even a small or seemingly random one.

As the name implies, with value-based decisions we have to assign a value to each piece of information we use relating to the choice we are trying to make. With eating it's easy to get ourselves stuck when we value physical health, feeling comfortable, satisfaction *and* weight loss. There are so many competing values, no wonder we get ourselves into such a mess!

Choice and meaning are linked to one another. What you are making anything mean in the moment will have an influence on the choice you end up making. Remember, we impose meaning on everything. If we stopped doing this, depression might move in. If, to you, overeating means you are weak-willed and a failure, what impact does that have on your ability to make choices? Usually, the all-or-nothing thinking comes in here; you will either promise yourself you'll be more disciplined, or you'll give up, believing there is no point because you're going to fail at some point anyway.

It's so important to question what you have made overeating mean about you. Again, you think this is just the truth about how you are, but it's not; it's the image of yourself you have constructed – your self-image and your identification with that image.

Responsible for our response

The whole point of this step is that you're consciously choosing how to react. Our initial reactions may be automatic, but when we notice this we can work through the method and choose how we want to respond to that initial reaction. This is, in fact, responsibility – our response-ability, or ability to respond.

Responsibility is often seen as synonymous with feeling burdened or under pressure. Usually it feels like this when you are taking on too much or taking responsibility for things that are not within your control. A common one is taking responsibility for how others feel. Yes, your behaviour may influence how someone feels, but you can't manage their emotional experience for them. Their ability to manage their feelings is their response-ability, not yours. You can strive relentlessly to protect someone from their feelings of anxiety, depression or anger, but it's exhausting to try to anticipate and manage all the factors that may be working against you. Parents try to protect their children from pain, but they can't wrap them up in cotton wool and keep them indoors. We all encounter painful experiences, so rather than trying to avoid them we'd be better off learning how to manage them.

Every time you berate yourself for your past overeating, you are taking responsibility for something that you cannot change. We can only be responsible for how we *respond* to the stuff that's beyond our control. The past is always beyond your control and the future only exists in your imagination. All you have is right now. Your responsibility, the ability to respond, is only now. Only now can you make a choice. You try to take responsibility for the future by promising yourself you'll only eat this and you won't eat that, but even the future isn't your responsibility.

Not yet anyway.

⌘

The RALIC Method
A Quick Guide

R for Recognise

Take a moment to stop and notice what is going on. This act alone interrupts the automatic thought patterns and awakens the part of you that has the ability to observe yourself. Starting with the words 'I recognise', write or say aloud what you recognise about the situation, the feelings you are experiencing and what you are believing and telling yourself about it. Pay attention to whether you are treating subjective beliefs as facts, e.g. 'I recognise this situation is horrible.' This would become, 'I recognise I am believing this situation to be horrible.'

A for Accept

Decide to stop fighting with reality. Go through your recognition statements and figure out how to accept them. Remember, you are only accepting this moment and you are only accepting what is already happening. Your mind may try to tell you that if you accept, you will keep experiencing this uncomfortable situation. But continually resisting the way things are usually creates more conflict and this will be what keeps you stuck. Try using the words 'Of course' when you are working through your statements, e.g. 'Of course I am experiencing an urge to overeat, this is what usually happens in these situations,' or 'Of course I am feeling this way, I need to feel it to move forwards.'

LI for Lean In

When the mind has stopped fighting and has become willing to recognise and accept, now you can feel your current reality. Mentally move towards the feelings, focusing on how they move and express within your body. There is not a 'right' way to do this. No one can tell you how this part is supposed to feel. It's less about doing anything and more about being in it. If it is a compulsive urge to eat that you are experiencing, you have an opportunity to listen to it and learn about it. The mind tries to tell you that you should be doing this or that when you experience this feeling, but what about deciding to experience it and really getting into the centre of what this sensation is?

C for Choose

In the first three stages you let go of trying to control your circumstances, thoughts and feelings by accepting they are there and being willing to experience them. Now you have an opportunity to choose your response. Sometimes this will be choosing an action, other times it may be about choosing an attitude or to shift your focus. You have embraced the willingness to be present; to be where life is actually happening – in the here and now. This means your next decision can be made from a place of presence, rather than a compulsive desire to escape. Be careful about starting the method with an idea about what choice you believe you should be making. Be open to discovering that you are capable of knowing what a wise choice may be for you.

⌘

Chapter 13

Troubleshooting the RALIC Method

'Nothing will work unless you do.'
– Maya Angelou

I hoped that by sharing the RALIC method with my clients they too would use it to find freedom from their eating struggles. I soon discovered how presumptuous it was to assume that what helps some will help everyone, so I quickly learned to temper my evangelism about the method. When I mentioned to a fellow therapist that I was presenting a technique in this book called the RALIC method she screwed up her face and told me, 'I'm sorry, I just don't like that stuff. It doesn't sit right with me.' I hadn't told her anything except the name, but I imagine she thought it sounded like it was going to be prescriptive and preachy; a just-do-these-steps-and-you'll-be-cured kind of thing. When you put big ideas into four steps it sounds very simple and straightforward, but of course, it isn't. Just like with diets, some people have a tendency to blame themselves when they struggle to make the method work for them. This is something I hope to avoid.

The whole point of putting big ideas into four steps is to have something that is consistent when life isn't; to have a structure we can reach for when we are overwhelmed by our own thoughts and to find our way back from compulsivity and unconsciousness.

Structure gives you something to hold onto when your mind is spinning and your thinking is being clouded by heightened emotions. RALIC is more than a method, it's an intention and a philosophy for how to live a more present life. Sometimes, when life stresses take us over, it's easy to lose sight of this. Many of my clients are very receptive to giving the RALIC method a go, but they get frustrated when they hit obstacles, or if nothing seems to be changing. I want to use this chapter to address some of the very common challenges and difficulties that people face when learning to apply the method.

Problem 1: 'I never seem to catch myself in the right moment to RALIC. I always miss it.'

I know you're not happy about your overeating and you probably have a difficult relationship with your body too. Trying to change this has been your battle for a long time, so of course you are hoping the RALIC method will help you fix this. Because this feels like the biggest problem in your life, it is a highly emotive subject for you. Some of your behaviours have become deeply ingrained habits so, when you are in your pre-binge state, it may be hard to find the mental space needed to stop, recognise and work through the steps. You are trying to do something brand new, at a time when the urge to allow yourself to go unconscious with food is strong. In these moments you don't want to be present with reality or work through some stupid method.

If you keep planning to use the method for your food choices, but keep forgetting or don't do it, I would invite you to consider using RALIC in other areas of your life first. I'm going to take a stab in the dark and assume the rest of your life isn't perfect either, so what are the challenges that have less resistance around them than your relationship with food? Often, the way you do one thing is the way you do everything. Becoming free to make choices in other areas of your life will help you to become freer when it comes to choosing what you eat.

When you read that last paragraph you may have thought *But I want to fix my relationship with food first because that's the main problem*. You may feel like you don't have the time, energy or inclination to work on the other stuff. If so, that could be all-or-nothing thinking creeping in. Working through the RALIC method will challenge your all-or-nothing thinking so, if you use the method to become less all-or-nothing in other areas of your life first, you may be able to translate this to food decisions more easily.

Do you have an annoying co-worker? Maybe you've just had an argument with a friend? Now might be the time to Recognise, Accept, Lean In and make a Choice. It's easier to use the smaller moments to practise. In a non-food-related situation, working through the method might look something like this:

- *Recognise* – 'I recognise my friend cancelled our plans an hour before we were supposed to meet...I recognise I am now facing an evening alone...I recognise I am feeling hurt, disappointed and angry...I recognise I am not believing the reason she gave me...I recognise I am believing that she doesn't want to see me...I recognise I am telling myself she shouldn't have cancelled on me...'

- *Accept* – 'Of course I am believing she doesn't want to see me, that's what I often think when it comes to other people. Of course I may never know for sure why she cancelled, so of course I'm going to fill in the gaps. Of course I feel hurt, disappointed and angry, and I can let myself feel what I feel. I accept this moment.'

- *Lean In* – Decide not to run or distract from the moment. Sit in it. Notice the sensations in your body; notice how they move and respond to your attention. Feel the hurt, disappointment and anger. Embrace and accept them simply because they exist right now.

- *Choose* – You may choose to remind yourself it is your interpretation of the event that is causing your feelings, more so than the event itself. You may decide to suggest another time to meet, or allow yourself to consciously indulge your emotions for a while.

If you keep forgetting to use the method in situations related to eating, it's worth getting more comfortable and familiar with the steps first. Trying to do something brand new, while in the midst of feeling out of control with food, is a tough ask. As mentioned earlier, using RALIC after a session of overeating can be a good place to start. Working the steps on the way you react to your overeating can be an opportunity to create a shift in perspective, and any shift can help to destabilise the overall cycle.

Problem 2: 'I don't know how to recognise when eating is problematic for me. I'm so confused.'

Recognition requires the willingness to shine a light on parts of yourself that you may not even be aware of yet. There may be a lot of confusion about when you cross the line from 'normal' into 'compulsive' eating. You tell yourself you'll just have one cookie and then you eat five; is that a problem? At what point did it tip over into feeling like you weren't making a choice anymore?

You also need to be honest with yourself about whether you are eating enough overall to keep restriction at bay. If you are, then you get to decide what eating is problematic and what's okay with you. Focusing on how your body feels when it comes to what you eat may be the best place to start. This is where the intuitive eating principles can support you.

If you keep struggling with this step, I wonder if there could be anything lurking outside of your awareness, on the fringe of your consciousness? If you are really struggling to understand your patterns, you might consider booking a short course of counselling sessions to have some time with an impartial person who is trained to help you understand the things you're struggling to see. This doesn't need to be someone who specialises in eating problems, just an empathic, skilled counsellor who can facilitate self-exploration and help you to increase your self-awareness. A short course of four to six sessions, with a clear agreement about using the time to understand your patterns around food and the thoughts you have about your body, may bring enough clarity for you to do this step more effectively. Starting counselling can be a bit like beginning a running programme. When you fully commit to either, you often notice big gains at the start. I'm a big fan of long-term counselling if you can access it, but I think the benefits of even a handful of sessions are often underestimated.

Problem 3: 'Stop telling me to accept my body. I can't accept it and I need to lose weight.'

I hear you. No one should be telling you what you are supposed to do when it comes to your body, and that includes me telling you to accept it. Perhaps you are in a bigger body that makes navigating through life difficult. It may be that you are falling into the trap of believing that body acceptance means nothing changes. Accepting your body means the way you feel towards your body changes. A better relationship with your body often means you feel better able to look after it.

RALIC is not about reaching a final destination of body acceptance; it's about this moment and this moment only because life is made up of a series of current moments. Body acceptance often waxes and wanes. Some days you may feel more accepting, others you won't. If, in the moment, any form of body acceptance seems unfathomable to you, recognise this and then do the work on accepting how difficult it feels for you to accept your body. Acceptance doesn't mean forcing yourself to feel something that you don't. Always remember that you don't have to accept your body. You may feel liberated if you can, but believing it's another thing you should be doing may lead to you feeling even worse about yourself.

Problem 4: 'Leaning in is unbearable. It makes me feel worse and worse.'

My client Daisy described a sense of spiralling into a hole whenever she tried to lean in to her feelings. In this hole, she felt like someone who was worthless and that she deserved to be punished. She would then feel an urge to punish herself by overeating to the point of feeling sick. This kept happening whenever she tried to lean in.

When I asked her about her feelings, she told me, 'I just feel like I need to punish myself.' While this was her truth, it was also her interpretation of her emotions. Whenever she felt these sensations, they were accompanied by thoughts that, to her, meant there was something very wrong with who she was and she deserved to be punished for it. Daisy was the daughter of an alcoholic mother and had endured an abusive and neglectful childhood. She walked around with a very critical voice in her head, constantly telling her she was useless and worthless. Leaning in was hard because, when she did, she felt like a terrible person who deserved to be hurt. Eating was a way of escape, of achieving temporary relief from the self-shaming thoughts, as well as a way of satisfying her urge to punish herself.

Daisy's identity and self-image was of someone who was never good enough and deserved bad things. Because she was not able to separate the shaming thoughts from who she was, there was work to be done first around her identity and improving her ability to observe herself. For now, I suggested that she kept working stage one – recognising. This meant, whenever she could, stopping and simply recognising what was happening, e.g. 'I recognise I am believing I am worthless...I recognise I am telling myself I should be punished...I recognise I am feeling anxious...' Using the full RALIC method needed to be postponed until she could observe her experience without feeling overwhelmed.

If leaning in feels overwhelming to you, ask yourself what you are making your feelings mean. See if you can challenge these and find alternative, softer meanings that are less shame inducing. If this is too difficult to manage on your own, it may be time to speak to a counsellor or appropriate professional.

Problem 5: 'I keep choosing to binge. Help!'

If it feels like every time you get to the choice part, you keep choosing to binge, then there are a couple of things I would urge you to consider. What are you calling a binge? Everyone's idea about what constitutes a binge varies. One slice of cake? Probably not a binge. What about two, three or four? At what point does it become a binge? You may have a clear idea that x amount of food equals a binge, but it's probably more to do with how you feel about what you've eaten. It may be that what your body wants and what you think you need are in conflict. You may need to work through the method on the conflict itself.

If you keep getting to the last step and choosing to overeat to the point of discomfort, my question would be this – does it feel like you can choose not to binge when you get to the choice stage? If it doesn't feel possible then it won't be an option for you. Either the deprivation response is being triggered, or you're feeling like you need to escape the discomfort of the current moment. You could try spending a bit more time in the leaning in stage. This step helps you to develop the ability to stay with what is. When you know you can handle uncomfortable feelings and you can recognise and accept the thoughts that accompany them, you get to choose what you want those feelings to mean to you.

During my recovery, I practised responding differently to my feelings by allowing them and then consciously choosing not to catastrophise them. I would tell myself that *because I've had this feeling so often in the past, of course it's going to come up now. It doesn't mean anything has gone wrong.* When I started doing this I gradually stopped believing that I had to keep chasing away my feelings of agitation by eating. I knew I still could if I wanted to, but I got to the point where I didn't want to be doing that anymore. I was fed up with using food to try to control my experience of life and fed up of feeling so bad about myself.

If you are at the point where you no longer want to use food to escape and you are ready to relinquish control, then let this be the intention that you bring to the method. Like with intuitive eating, an intention can support you to move in the direction you want to go. Unrealistic intentions will mean you keep setting yourself up to fall down again, and this will only serve to confirm all those critical beliefs you keep having about yourself. An intention to be in control of your food intake may backfire into repeated bouts of losing control, but an intention to make choices that honour your physical, mental, emotional and social needs will support you in making decisions that feel right for you.

If you get to the choice part and keep getting anxious and confused, spend some time getting clear about what your intentions are for using the method. If your intention is to become an intuitive eater, then you can look for choices that would support this intention while at the same time recognising that you don't have to become an intuitive eater. You don't have to change your eating, or do anything differently. Even if there are consequences that you don't enjoy, you still get to choose.

Maybe you wish you could take the RALIC method and immediately be able to use it to make all the 'right' choices. It may seem like, in the beginning, all the RALIC method is doing is bringing more awareness to your self-sabotaging decisions. This will test your patience. There may be some blocks that need clearing from your blind spots. The method enables you to notice the parts of you that are driving your compulsive eating and offers a way of becoming more connected to those parts that are currently being pushed outside of your awareness. We often think we know ourselves better than we really do, but when we keep recognising the bits we normally avoid, we become more open and self-aware.

I don't believe my personal therapy cured my overeating, but it did get me to a place of greater awareness and understanding. It was from this awareness that I could figure out what I needed to do to become free. I didn't recover until after I left therapy. Would I have managed to recover if I hadn't had therapy? I can't say for certain, but I imagine not.

You want to change your eating, but to do this in a lasting way, *you* need to change. In order to change your behaviour, the way you view yourself has to shift. If you keep seeing things the same way, you'll keep doing things the same way. If you keep getting frustrated with the food choices that you make after RALICing, then leave the food for a bit and just work through the method in other areas of your life.

There may be something going on in your life that needs to change first, before your eating can. It's easier and more convenient to convince yourself that you would be a different person if you lost the weight. You want to do that first because you believe that then you will be more confident and comfortable with who you are. That version of you will be able to address the things in your life that you are currently putting off or avoiding. What are the parts of your life you would rather not address yet? If you are avoiding some bigger issues in your relationships, job or family, you may end up using food as a way to continue doing this.

⌘

Chapter 14

The RALIC Life

'Whatever the present moment contains,
accept it as if you had chosen it.
Always work with it, not against it.'
– Eckhart Tolle

RALIC is more than just a way to change your relationship with food; it's a way of changing your relationship with life itself. Your struggle with food and body image may seem like a big issue in your life, maybe even the biggest issue, but what does this tell you about your life in general? This book may be about eating and how you feel in your body, but consider how these patterns show up in other areas of your life.

There are certain topics that come up again and again with my clients, so they seem to be fairly universal among those of us who struggle with food and body image. These themes are self-worth; control; fear of life; boundaries and freedom. As part of your commitment to increasing your self-awareness, it may be worth spending some time considering these themes throughout the different parts of your life.

Never good enough

Low self-worth can be a vicious spiral that's hard to get out of. The roots are laid down early in life by internalising the reactions of those around you towards you. If you had a stressed, impatient or neglectful parent you may have internalised a belief that nothing you do is ever good enough and that people are often unhappy around you or with you. Your young mind wouldn't have had the sophisticated thinking required to understand that someone else's stress, impatience or neglect was a lot less to do with you and a lot more to do with them.

If you believe nothing you do is good enough, you might go either of two ways. You could feel paralysed and depressed, believing that there is no point in trying when it's never going to be good enough anyway. Or you strive and push yourself to keep doing better in the hope that one day you'll feel like it's (or you are) enough. The third option is that you'll swing between the two – pushing then crashing, anxiety then depression; the all and the nothing, which develops into an all-or-nothing mindset.

The reason I call it a spiral is because it keeps getting reinforced. Each time you try and fail, your self-esteem gets lower and lower. Each time you are motivated to do things differently, each time you decide to take control of the situation, you raise your expectations. You make big promises to yourself and maybe to others too. Invariably, you can't live up to this unrealistic image you've created of yourself, so when the image collapses your self-worth takes another hit, knocking you back into a hole of despair.

Being seen

Self-care often conjures up images of bubble baths, holidays and manicures, but it's so much more than this. When you are caring for someone else, it isn't about pampering them. Caring for someone is just that, caring. 'I care about you.' What happens when you say those words to yourself? 'I care about you.' They might ring hollow. Find a mirror, look yourself right in your eyes and say those words aloud.

Eye contact is very powerful even, or perhaps especially, when it's your own. Being looked right in the eyes means we're being seen, and being seen is the first step to feeling connected. Many of us feel disconnected from ourselves. So spending some time seeing ourselves and deliberately being kinder with the self-talk is a great way to start reconnecting to ourselves.

We feel validated by being seen and understood and we can feel angry and hurt when others don't do this. We can also make it mean there is something inherently wrong with us. When we are waiting for others to give to us what we are unable or unwilling to give to ourselves we are going to be waiting a long time – even if they are giving it to us, we won't be able to feel it or trust it. Robert Holden in his book *Shift Happens* suggests that the things we want people to give to us are the things we are not giving ourselves. If you want more love, be more loving. If you want to feel understood, be more understanding.

Letting go (again!)

I've talked a lot about control already, but she is a sneaky madam who knows how to creep back in unnoticed. For a long time I knew that when I focused on controlling my eating for weight loss, bingeing always followed. In my journey towards recovery, each time I had a break in my bingeing, my weight would start to come down. I would get excited, over-focus on my food again, feel guilty if I thought I'd overeaten and then I was back bingeing before I knew it. But it was so insidious. Even when I wasn't trying to diet I was trying to figure out with my thinking brain how much I should be eating. Subtle judgements would sneak in. Judgements like *I've eaten quite a lot today so I'd better be a bit more careful tomorrow*, or *I had some chocolate at lunchtime so I shouldn't really have anything else that's sugary today*. The thing was, when I learned to trust my appetite and eat more intuitively it always balanced out on its own. As soon as my critical thinking got involved it all fell apart again.

Of course we have to engage our thinking minds to some degree when deciding what to eat. If you were listening to your body and feeling like you wanted a burger and salad, but this wasn't available, then there has to be the ability to negotiate a suitable alternative. If you're feeling hungry at 4 pm, but you know you'll be going out for a three course meal at 7 pm, that information may be considered when you are deciding if or what to eat at that time. On the other hand, if you know it's going to be a long gap before you eat again, you may consciously push further past fullness than you normally would.

Using the RALIC method in these situations can help you to make a choice about what to do. When there has been so much judgement and confusion around what and how much to eat, developing the ability to recognise, accept and lean in to those feelings will help you gain clarity in your thinking, as well as connecting you to your feelings. Confusion was a big one for me, but I kept accepting that *of course I'm going to feel confused, I've been struggling with this for years!* Accepting my confusion released me from it. It took the pressure off and I felt free to make the best choices I was capable of making in the moment.

If anything were to yank me out of my recovered state, it would be trying to control again. I have to make a conscious decision over and over again to relinquish control over that which is beyond my control and this is not just with food. A big one for me is surrendering to the fact that I can't fix anyone; that's not in my control either. If I believed it was my job to ensure a client's recovery, I would be carrying an enormous weight on my shoulders. I wouldn't be able to do my job properly; it would become about me and my need to feel like I was doing a good job. This is what happens when we try to control what we can't – we often make things worse.

Writing this book and putting it out there has been another lesson for me in letting go. I just had to write the book that was in my heart and let it go. I poured my soul onto these pages and I believe in every word and yet, I have to accept there are going to be people who will not like it, there are going to be people who will not like me and there are going to be those who my message simply won't connect to. That's okay, but the only reason it's okay is because it has to be.

I wonder what else you may be trying to control that is a constant source of frustration for you. I once heard frustration described as anger + powerlessness. You may be angry that something isn't the way it is 'supposed' to be, and you may feel powerless if it's something you cannot control. What do you need to recognise and accept, so that you can move forwards?

If other parts of your life are chaotic, it's unlikely you are going to find a peaceful state with the food.

For some, it's incredibly scary to acknowledge that most of what happens in life is beyond our control. Maybe this wasn't a revelation to you; perhaps life usually feels out of control. If life feels big and scary and full of terrible things, why wouldn't you want to escape it, at least for a while, with food?

Even though what happens is often beyond our control, we *can* work on how we want to respond to the twists and turns of life. When we are struggling with something we can't control, if we don't find a way to let that stuff go then we will continue to suffer. We don't want to accept it, because we think we know how things should be. We think we know what will make us happy and we're willing to be thoroughly miserable in order to prove it.

Remember, there's two parts to our reality – what's going on outside of us, and our response, which happens inside of us. The good news is that your response can be under your influence. You may think that's not true because you can't stop the horrible thoughts and feelings you have about your body. True, you can't stop these thoughts because they exist physically in the neural networks of your brain and are inter-connected with your emotional chemistry. They are events in and of themselves. However, your response is more than just your automated thoughts and feelings. We can deliberately choose to develop new thoughts and feelings to support a new perspective, but it doesn't work if you keep using up your energy fighting with the old. Let them be. Recognise, accept and lean in to them, but keep bringing yourself back to the truth, which is that they are shadows of the past and have no meaning that is separate from the one you decide to bestow on them, right now, in this moment.

Those things that are going on outside of you are not you. I know that may sound self-evident, but so often we assume things are about us that are not actually about us. Other people's behaviour is a classic example. If you are prone to social anxiety, you may believe that if someone is being a bit withdrawn or quiet, it means that the person finds you boring or irritating. When we don't know why someone said or did something, it's only human nature to try to find a possible reason for it. We want to make sense of our world and we do this by imposing meaning on everything, but we base our meaning on how we view ourselves and our place in the world. Our conclusions are always biased and often unreliable.

Boundaries and rules

We have our experiences and others have theirs. As we navigate around and interact with each other, we are constantly colliding with other people's experience and sometimes they come crashing into ours. Good boundaries are about knowing where you end and the other person begins. If your boundaries are porous, you will absorb other people's emotions and frustrations, and carry them around along with your own. This can feel overwhelming. If your boundaries are constantly moving around, people won't know where they are. They'll keep pushing against you until they know where the limits are. This means you have to be pushed to your limit before you feel able to tell them to back off!

Children are excellent at quickly sussing out where the boundaries are. If your boundaries are inconsistent (e.g. sometimes tantrums work to get what the child wants and sometimes they don't), they'll learn that their best shot of getting a desired outcome is to keep pushing because they know the boundaries sometimes move.

This doesn't mean you need to have rigid, inflexible boundaries. That's another manifestation of the black-and-white thinking that we're trying to move away from. We need to find a middle ground here as well. If you often agree to things, but feel a bit resentful later, you may want to consider your relationship to boundaries. If your boundaries are weak or insecure, you'll often find yourself wishing that other people would stop making so many demands of you. You may even blame others for always asking and not thinking of you more, but remember that if you want others to think of you more, then you may need to start thinking about you more first.

Boundaries and rules can become muddled. A rule tends to mean something is acceptable or not acceptable, good or bad. A rule is: *Do not eat after 8 pm. If I do, that's bad and now I've broken the rule.* A boundary is structure, as opposed to law, and its job is to protect and support. Perhaps eating late doesn't make you feel as good as you do when you eat a bit earlier. If you do eat late, it's not the end of the world. You may remember that it doesn't feel good, or you may realise that actually, you feel fine. If you prefer not to eat late, you can simply think about what you might need to help you to eat a bit earlier. Do you need to make some time for yourself, or have a plan in place? The whole point of a boundary is to feel safe.

The whole point of a rule is compliance, because it's what you should do. Boundaries give you space to move around within them; rules pin you down. We want to feel safe and we want to feel free. Rules sometimes feel safer, but can cost you your freedom. Having no rules or boundaries may make you free, but can cost you your sense of safety.

Making mistakes

In the process of becoming an intuitive eater, you'll start to learn about the ebbs and flows of your hunger. As you become more in tune with your body you'll become better at predicting what you're going to need and want in the near future. Structure around your eating starts to develop and with structure come new, more supportive habits. When new behaviours and attitudes towards food are repeated, they start to move from value-based decisions to habits. Now it's 'just the way you are.'

This is a process. When food has become such a difficult area, be prepared to make some 'mistakes.' I use inverted commas here because are they really mistakes? When a child learns to walk, is it a mistake every time they fall down? Of course not. Learning to pick yourself up and resetting your intention on what you are trying to accomplish is a necessary part of getting better at something. How you recover from slips, trips and falls will determine how you progress. It's not a race. There isn't a finish line where you finally go, 'I've made it! My body is how I want it and my eating is just right.' Your relationship to food and body is a journey. A journey that mirrors your life. What are the lessons that life is trying to teach you? To answer that question, just look at what keeps cropping up. Life seems to throw the same things at us again and again. Now might be the time to stop and listen.

When something that we want becomes a habit, we free up energy to use elsewhere. When we are not living in alignment with what we value, misery can flourish.

A life without regret

Looking back to the end of life exercise from chapter two: when your time on this planet is coming to an end, what do you want to see when you look back over your life? If you start to think about what you would see, rather than what you would want to see, stop. Breathe. What do you *want* to see? Sometimes we don't like thinking about what we want. It's too painful if we don't believe it's possible, so we want to escape the pain. What do we do when we want to escape? Eat.

Death is such a strange concept. Even though we know our lives are just a flash in eternity it feels like we've always existed. We can't imagine what it's like to die. Early on in our lives we learn that death will take us one day. Most of us don't think about that too much, but we have that information in our minds, maybe in a dark crevice, or maybe at the forefront. Just because we rarely acknowledge our mortality it doesn't mean it isn't a driving factor in the way we live our lives.

Bronnie Ware, a palliative care nurse, spent a great deal of time with people who were approaching death. She spoke with these people and recorded the top five regrets of the dying. These were:

1. I wish I'd had the courage to live a life true to myself, not the life others expected of me.
2. I wish I hadn't worked so hard.
3. I wish I'd had the courage to express my feelings.
4. I wish I had stayed in touch with my friends.
5. I wish I had let myself be happier.

That last one really gets me. So often I meet people who are postponing happiness until they feel like they have earned it. It's like we don't believe we deserve to be happy with our imperfect lives and wobbly bodies. This is the most pervasive and destructive message in our diet-and-appearance-obsessed culture. If you have absorbed this message and it's hard to let it go, it doesn't make you shallow. Many of my clients beat themselves up for caring so much about this stuff, but you have been taught to care. We are social creatures with a need to belong. When society says you have to do this, or you have to look like that, in order to be accepted very few of us are immune to that kind of pressure.

If you continue to look outside for evidence that you are finally good enough, you may be waiting for a long time. You are not broken. Perhaps your relationship with food and your body needs to heal, but you, as a human being on this planet, do not have to change to become more valuable or worthy of care.

We often talk about recovery as a journey, as if there is a point where you can finally label yourself a 'recovered binge eater', but life is only ever happening now. This means that each time you eat from a place of presence, each time you choose to nourish yourself (physically and emotionally), you move away from the binge eater identity. You become somebody who is connected and free.

This person exists in you now.

Set them free.

⌘

Exercises and Resources

I wanted to collate and include a list of exercises and resources you can turn to for support as you move towards a new relationship with food and your body. Change often comes through new experiences, so if you are feeling stuck you can keep returning to this section and try one of the exercises. These are some of the exercises I use in my practice and some resources I recommend.

Gratitude list – *perspective, body image, emotions*

Sending your brain off to look for things to appreciate is an effective way to gain some perspective and is an excellent habit to develop. The more you do it, the easier it becomes, and you may find you start noticing things that make you feel good without even trying.

Have a notebook and pen beside your bed. Every night, before you go to sleep, write down three things you are grateful for. If possible, try to find things that happened that day. If it feels as if you've had such a bad day that you can't find anything, then go bigger and broader. You may be grateful for your home, job or health. Perhaps there is a person you are thankful to have in your life. Commit to doing this every day for a period of time and see how you feel. You could do a month, or you may decide to do it until you have filled your notebook. Consistent gratitude practice can increase feelings of happiness and connectedness.

To make this exercise body image specific, write down three things you are grateful for about your body. Many of these can be about what your body does or can do. Don't be afraid to shoot for the obvious here. Just because your body has done these things every day for your whole life doesn't make them any less miraculous.

Mirror work – *perspective, self-acceptance*

Go look at your reflection. Make eye contact with yourself and really see yourself. Talk to yourself as you would talk to someone you cared about. Hearing our own voice and gazing into our own eyes can help us to feel more connected with ourselves. This can be a very powerful exercise; what do you want to tell yourself? Instead of just thinking about it, do it face-to-face.

Set an intention – *post-binge, perspective, avoiding restriction*

This one is especially good if you are feeling confused about what to eat or you have just binged. You don't need rules, simply an intention about where to put your focus. You may set an intention to be totally present with your next meal; intend to pause, breathe and check in with your body the next time you eat. You may intend to focus on one of the intuitive eating principles, such as discovering your satisfaction or finding some joyful movement. You may work through the RALIC steps and find the right intention for you during the last stage (Choose).

I hate my...but... – *body image, self-acceptance*

When you notice you are saying mean things to yourself, add a 'but' on the end and find a kinder ending to the thought. This is not about arguing with your critical thoughts or trying to force them away (this usually doesn't work). It's making a conscious effort to create some balance to these thoughts. If you catch sight of yourself in a shop window and think *God, I look awful* you can add a 'but' onto the end of that thought and find a kinder, more generous ending to that sentence. It might become *God, I look awful...but my body feels strong*. Or you may choose an ending that has nothing to do with your body at all, such as *God, I look awful...but I'm doing well in my work project at the moment*.

Guided meditations – *post-binge, self-acceptance*

There are so many great body scan guided visualisations out there. You can trawl through YouTube and try a few out. I like Yoga Nidra by Lizzie Hill (YouTube).

Spend time with yourself – *perspective, self-awareness*

Schedule some time to be with yourself. Walking is one way to do this. Leave your phone at home and walk for the sake of walking, just to be with your thoughts and check in with yourself, even if it's a quick lap around the block.

If you are travelling around, take out your headphones or switch off the car stereo and see what happens. We live in a world that tends to chase quietness away, but it's in the moments of peace and quiet that we can hear ourselves and tune into what's going on inside us.

Keep a food diary – *increasing self-awareness, learning hunger/fullness cues*

Approach this one cautiously. Food logging can be closely associated with dieting, so I don't recommend it for everyone. Some people may find it a useful way to stay present with food, or may want to log how certain foods make them feel. When used well, food diaries can be a tool for increasing your self-awareness. I highly recommend an app called *Rise Up and Recover*. There are no calories or portion sizes, and you don't see what you ate earlier, unless you download the PDF, so it's less triggering than other food recording methods. There is also a space for comments so you can use a hunger scale or make a couple of notes about how you are feeling.

Journalling – *self-awareness, perspective, intention-setting*

Taking time to self-reflect and getting your thoughts out on paper can help you connect to your experience and find some perspective. You can simply pour out a stream of consciousness straight onto the page; this is a great way to clear your head. Journalling prompts are particularly helpful if you are trying to challenge or understand your thinking. You may want to journal while you are working through the RALIC method if you have the space to do so. Writing it out can help to cement the stages in your mind.

Here are some other journalling prompts you could consider using:

- What is the kindest interpretation of this moment?
- Write a letter of friendship to your body.
- What areas of my life are feeling like a struggle?
- What do I want my relationship with food to look like?
- How can I look after myself today/tomorrow?
- What intentions can I set to support me?

Plan a binge – *self-awareness, emotional eating, breaking the cycle*

This one is going to sound a bit strange, but hear me out. Try planning a binge. That's right, deciding beforehand that you will binge. Plan it the day before, not on the day. Write down when and where you are planning to binge, record everything you are planning to eat and make it generous. Planning food has always been associated with trying to eat less in the past; you believe that if you plan food, it should be because you are trying to be 'good', right? The thought of planning to binge in advance may feel very uncomfortable.

There is such a well-worn cycle to bingeing. You feel strong urges to do it, and experience a sense of being out of control. When it is planned and you do it, regardless of whether you feel like it or not, it's harder to go unconscious and you have a completely different emotional experience of bingeing. Being out of control doesn't come into it, so it confuses the cycle. There is a lot you can learn about yourself through giving this one a go, so it's worth doing some journalling around the experience.

And-and – *interrupting patterns, food choices*

If you are experiencing an urge for a particular food you normally binge on, to help you stay conscious try having the food, but pair it with a nutritionally dense food that you wouldn't normally eat with it. This might look like having an apple and chocolate bar at the same time or eating raspberries with ice cream. This protects you against the deprivation reaction and brings a greater consciousness to your choices.

Books to read

Body Positive Power by Megan Jayne Crabbe (Vermilion)

Body Respect by Linda Bacon (BenBella Books)

Bodies by Susie Orbach (Profile Books)

Fat is a Feminist Issue by Susie Orbach (Arrow Books)

Health at Every Size by Linda Bacon (BenBella Books)

Intuitive Eating by Evelyn Tribole and Elyse Resch (St Martin's Griffin)

Just Eat It by Laura Thomas (Bluebird)

Shift Happens by Robert Holden (Hay House Publishing)

The F*ck It Diet by Caroline Dooner (Harper Collins)

The Willpower Instinct by Kelly McGonigal (Avery Publishing Group Inc.)

Women, Food and God by Geneen Roth (Simon and Schuster Ltd)

Find a community – *support*

You don't need to do this alone. There are many spaces online to find support. I recommend the Intuitive Eating Support Group page on Facebook. Below are some Instagram accounts that are congruent with the message of this book.

If you are interested in therapy groups, please get in touch via my website www.thebingeeatingtherapist.com

You can also check out my YouTube channel, The Binge Eating Therapist, for weekly videos containing thought provoking content related to binge eating recovery.

Instagram accounts to follow (an updated list can be found at www.thebingeeatingtherapist.com in the resources section)

@the_binge_eating_therapist @aaronfloresrdn @abeautifulmind4me @a_body_well_fed @annamarie.rd @benourishedpdx @beyond_the_binge @body_acceptance_collective @bodybravecanada @bodyimage_therapist @bodyimagewithbri @body_peace_liberation @bodyposipanda @bodypositivephd @bopo.boy @bravebodylove @brokefatgirl @bulimiafree @carolynviggh @champagneandcurves @chr1styharrison @chubstr @concentriccounselling @cozibae @ditchthatdiet @dranitajohnston @drclaudiafelty @drcolleenreichmann @drsarahcairns @emmymbrunner @evelyntribole @fatpositivefertility @foodandpsych @fyeahmfabello @geneenroth @ginjaswagger @gogochristie @harri_rose_ @haes_studentdoctor @healthlifestylist @healingcrayons @hopefulhorizons.ca @i_weigh @intuitive.dietitian.kosher @intuitivelylacey @isabelfoxenduke @isarobinson_ @jameelajamilofficial @jennafree__ @jenniferdigennaro @jennifer_rollin @joyateverysize @katewas_, @kristamurias @kristinabruce_coach @kylafoxrecovery @laurathomasphd @loveyourbody.babe @madeonagenerousplan @metabolism_recovery @mindbodyfood @mindfultherapyatx @mittendietitian @mollybcounseling @moreloveorg @mspsychotherapy @nalgonapositivitypride @nom_nomaste.llc @nourishandeat @nudenutritionrd @onelife_showup @ownitbabe @phelanwell @positivelypresent @rachelwcole @reallyjaybee @rebeccascritchfield @recoverwithmeda @reflectwholenesstherapy @reframebodylove @stephdodier @summerinnanen @Thebirdspapaya @thebodypositive @thecrankytherapist @the_eating_disorder_therapist @thefatedrecoverycoach @thefightforbeauty @thefuckitdiet @theintuitive_rd @thephitcoach @therapy_with_brooke @the.truthful.scoop @virgietovar @wearerebelfit @whatcan_Ichange @whole_embodied_therapist @with_this_body @_wobblybits_ @womenshealth.dietician @100daysoffoodfreedom

Hashtags to follow:

#allbodiesaregoodbodies #bingeeatinghelp #bingee-atingrecovery #bodyacceptance #bodyneutral #bodyneu-trality #bodypeace #bodypositivity #bodypositive #bopo #bopowarrior #bodyrespect #ditchthediet #edrecovery #fatpositiveprovider #foodisbeautiful #gentlenutrition #haes #healthateverysize #intuitiveeating #intuitiveeatingofficial #iweigh #livenownotwhen #mindfuleating #makepeacewith-food #makepeacewithyourplate #mindfuleatingtips #nodiet #nondiet #nondietapproach #nourishnotpunish #positive-bodyimage #ralicmethod #ralic #scalesareforfish #screwthes-cales #selfcare #selfacceptance #selfcompassion #selfloveisthe-bestlove #weightneutral #weightneutrality #youaintyourweight #yourbodyyourrules

Acknowledgements

Writing this book has been an extraordinary experience and one I would not have been able to manage on my own. There have been many others who have been on this journey with me and helped me to feel less alone.

Thank you to How2Become publishers for holding my hand through this process and keeping me accountable. Special mention to Jordan Cooke and Andi Atherton who patiently read every page and provided such valuable feedback. I have learned so much from you both.

To my copyeditors, Jen Bradly and Sandra Board, a big thank you for making me look like a real writer and for tidying up after me. Your astute suggestions have brought clarity to the vision of this book.

A special mention to Claire MacDonald for your enthusiasm and your willingness to bounce ideas around with me, and to Isa Robinson who generously gave up her time to read and fact check the chapter on intuitive eating and nutrition.

I would not be the psychotherapist I am today without my supervisors. These three wise women, Marie O'Sullivan, Tina Free and Kel O'Neil, each have their own unique strengths and continue to give me what I need so I can always be evolving my thinking about this work.

Words cannot do justice to my feelings of gratitude towards my network of fellow therapists. You are my extended family and my friends. To Roksana Paciepnik, your unwavering belief in this book has helped me during my dark moments of doubt. To Gareth Sammer, you are the kindest and most generous man

I know. To Denise Sims, who showed me that fortune favours the brave; I think I can let go of your coat tails now.

A shout out to my long-time friend, Nicki Glencross, who scooped me up in 2011 when my world had fallen apart, who saw me sink into the depths and cheered when I crawled my way out, crying tears of pride when she read this book. I love you Fordy.

And lastly, to the people who so generously allowed me to share their experiences in this book. You guys get the biggest thank you. Without people like you being willing to allow your stories to be told, binge eating will continue to remain the shameful secret.

About the Author

Sarah Dosanjh is a qualified psychotherapist and certified Transactional Analyst who trained at the Metanoia Institute and the National Centre for Eating Disorders. She meets with clients at her private practice in West London and also online. As well as seeing clients for individual sessions, she facilitates binge eating therapy groups.

Under the name 'The Binge Eating Therapist' she actively engages with eating disorder and body image communities on Instagram and launched her own YouTube channel of the same name in December 2019.

A couple of times a year she runs professional development workshops in London for fellow therapists and counsellors wanting to know more about how to work with clients who come for help with compulsive eating.

For more details or to work with Sarah please visit www.thebingeeatingtherapist.com

Made in the USA
Coppell, TX
12 February 2022

73485810R00118